Puffin Books

Editor: Kaye Webb

AJAX THE WARR

Mary Elwyn Patchett's childhood was the kind that many of us have dreamed about. She lived on a remote cattle station in the wild Australian bush, with plenty of freedom and masses of pets, including a boxing kangaroo named Matilda, ponies to ride, a possum, a snake, and three dogs of her own, Algy, Ben and Ajax.

This book is full of stories about all the animals, but it is wonderful Ajax who stands out from the rest, for he was a king among dogs. Mary found him as a defenceless orphan puppy and reared him by hand; in the end he grew into a fighter dog as big as a calf. He never played with other dogs and only just put up with humans, for all the love in his heart was fixed on Mary and twice he saved her from death.

Mary Elwyn Patchett is the author of two other Puffin books, *The Brumby* and *Come Home, Brumby*, but her own true adventures sometimes seem even more exciting than the ones in the novels.

For readers of eight and over.

Cover design by David Carl Forbes

Ajax The Warrior

Mary Elwyn Patchett

Illustrated by
Eric Tansley

Penguin Books

Penguin Books Ltd, Harmondsworth,
Middlesex, England
Penguin Books Australia Ltd, Ringwood,
Victoria, Australia

First published by Lutterworth Press 1953
Published in Puffin Books 1972

Made and Printed in Great Britain by
C. Nicholls & Company Ltd
The Philips Park Press, Manchester
Set in Linotype Pilgrim

For Bob, Barbara and Wentworth

Contents

1. Land of Lonely Adventure

From away back as far as I can remember I lived in the strange, wild land of the Australian bush until I was fifteen and went to boarding school. My memory dates back from when I was two, when I was badly burnt, and I never left my home for more than a few months until the time came for me to go to school.

Life on a cattle station was a lonely life, unless you were lucky enough to be one of a large family; but for me there were seldom other children to play with except when an occasional friend came to stay, or there were odd children around for a few weeks. I had an elder brother, but he went off to boarding school when I was very small, and only came home for the long holidays twice yearly, so in a way I was very much alone.

In another way I was not alone at all. I had my dogs, and a collection of Australian animals that ranged from a calf to a carpet snake called Kaa. My life was very busy indeed, and full of adventures, for these are a part of the great, lonely lands of Australia, with its rivers, that may one week be just a string of muddy pools, and the next a roaring torrent of yellow water seven miles wide.

It was a wild country and I loved it; I still do, from its gum trees with tall silver-and-mauve-streaked trunks, satin-smooth and shining in the moonlight, to the wide brown paddocks where the great herds of beef cattle roam and the little kangaroo rats make round nests from dried wisps of grass, and come bounding out like fur-covered balls of grey when you disturb them, zig-zagging like hares to throw off the coursing dogs; from the tree-fringed river, where the brown oblongs of resting platypuses dotted the dark waters beneath the trees, to where the possums gave their soft, ka ka kkkkaas, and the melancholy cry of a dingo filled the lonely moonlight and turned the vast emptiness of Australia into a land of ancient life, haunted by loneliness and hunger.

There were Christmases and birthdays for me just as there are for children everywhere – only my cake was smaller, and there were plates of bones and nuts and fruit for my guests! All year long there were regular happenings that were interesting to me, and in which I could sometimes take part. There were polo and picnic race meetings, an occasional circus and buckjumping show and regular country shows for stock and agriculture.

These shows were very important to stations like my home, Gunyan, because we had a stud of pure-bred Herefords, and our champions competed at many shows during the year, and we always exhibited all the new, imported stock. During the 1914 war we had a fine Hereford bull shipped from England. The ship he was in was torpedoed, but the bull was rescued although its journey took months, and by the time it arrived it cost over £3,000. Then the very night the bull reached Gunyan, after all these adventures, it broke through three strong fences and got into a lucerne patch, and died next day from overeating.

My father was not happy until another great, red, curly-haired beast arrived after a quieter voyage, and this one was stabled and groomed for the Inverell show. Show bulls have an enormous diet; besides greenstuffs they get boiled pumpkin and oil cakes, a dozen fresh eggs daily, and huge doses of castor oil which are supposed to make their coats curl!

Then when I was three I was allowed to compete in my first show. Two weeks beforehand the bulls were sent off in a huge van so that they would not walk the fat off themselves, and my fat brown pony Buck went along with them. I had spent weeks grooming him and feeding him lots of cracked corn and an occasional dose of the bull's castor oil – which he did not appreciate at all.

My parents and I started for Inverell a couple of days before the show opened, and I was very upset because I was not allowed to take the three dogs I had then. One was an ancient fox terrier called Bumpy, another was a pretty black Kelpie sheep dog, and there was a floppy pointer called Napoleon. However, I perked up, and was most impatient for the second day of the show, when the event for small children's ponies was to take place.

My great friend Lewis, who was the handyman round the station and always the person I depended on, brought Buck to me where I stood impatiently by the entrance to the show ring. Of course I rode without a saddle; there was just a cloth fastened on with a surcingle to keep me clean. Buck was very gay – being so full of cracked corn – and he curvetted his portly body about the ring where other children bobbed about on their ponies, warming them up too. I am told my father said to Lewis, rather uneasily:

'I must admit I'm a bit worried about my daughter's sportsmanship. If Buck doesn't get the blue ribbon she'll set up a terrible howl – she's sure to feel he's been insulted and that his feelings are hurt!'

Then the judge gave his orders and we all walked, trotted and cantered, and then lined up. In the end only Buck and a beautiful little black pony were left, and the judge walked forward and put the coveted blue ribbon round the black pony's neck. I'm glad to say I've only a hazy memory of what happened next, but I'm told I went very red in the face, leant over and shouted at the judge:

'Go away! Buck's the best – Buck *is* the best! Go away! You've hurt his feelings – take that nasty red ribbon away!'

Not very sportsmanlike! But the judge must have had children of his own, because he walked round and began talking to me. He put the red ribbon away in his pocket and took something else out which he fastened to the headband of Buck's bridle. I remember that I felt better. I felt better still when he took a wonderful object out of another pocket and fastened it on my small chest. I am told that I rode proudly round the ring, hastily followed by the real blue-ribbon winner from whom Buck had stolen all the applause, and then I cantered out of the exit gate and called my parents to look at the object that was fastened to Buck's forehead.

'Look!' I said proudly, 'Buck's got a special prize for having the nicest expression! And look here – 'I peered down at my meagre chest – '*I* got this one for being a good rider!'

Buck's noble brow wore a heart-shaped ticket with a picture of the fat lady from the side-show on one side, and a fortune for those born in February on the other; on my chest was a beautiful blue disc with a magic inscription in gold that said 'Champion Buff Orpington Hen'.

My mother said: 'Apparently the judge is a man who seldom empties his pockets!'

But I was delighted and said: *I* think that the judge is the kindest man in the world!'

2. Algy

Through all the adventures that happened in my childhood, and they ranged from helping to trap a horse-thief to nearly losing my life through three wolves that had escaped from a circus, I had three faithful and deeply loved companions, and the first of these was Algy, who must have come to me when I was about five. Algy was a bulldog, and I had been promised a bulldog pup for a long time before my parents were able to get one for me, because in those days there were not many of them in Australia.

Algy was an entrancing pup. He was only a few weeks old when he came a long rail and road journey all by himself, from the Queensland town of Warwick to Gunyan, near the border town of Texas. The river, the Severn, made the border between New South Wales and Queensland, so that if you wished you could practically stand with one foot in each state. The nearest rail station was forty miles away, and as a motor lorry was going to this station, Inglewood, to collect some goods, my father arranged for Algy to be sent that day. He told the driver to leave plenty of room for the pup in the truck, as bulldogs were such big fellows.

I hardly slept a wink the night before Algy was due to arrive; in fact everyone was excited, for most of the station hands had never seen a bulldog either. Presently we heard the truck in the distance, and soon it pulled up in front of the house, and the driver was grinning all over his face.

'It's a good thing you sent the big lorry, boss,' he called to my father. 'He's a savage brute – and what a size!'

Dancing about at the back of the truck, I could hardly wait for it to be opened so that I would get the first glimpse of my bulldog. But the driver walked round from the front with something in his hand, saying:

'Well, here he is!'

And there he was, the fattest, tiniest pup, all wrinkles, with a wee white, square-jawed face, floppy jowls, and a black button of a nose – and he weighed just three pounds. One half of his head was a sort of blackish-grey, and the rest of him was white, and there was a permanent kink in his tail. I could hold him in one hand. When I put him on the ground he tried to sniff at an ant, his nose was so far back he had almost to stand on his head, and his wobbly legs gave way and he fell on his nose. He was the dearest baby.

Algy soon grew from a chubby pup into a great big dog, weighing nearly five stone, with a massive chest and gentle, loving ways. He had plenty of affection from my family, yet his bulldog heart must have had some emptiness our love could not fill. The first time I realized this was when he trotted in from the garden with a strange creature held very gently between his drooling jaws. He came up to me, looking immensely pleased with himself, and put what he was carrying very gently in my lap. It was a tiny tortoise! Goodness knows where he had found it, perhaps on the river bank, perhaps on the dampish earth round the water tanks. It was not much bigger than a penny and quite black, and it reared its head and began scurrying round my lap. I helped it to the floor and it ran a little way, with Algy trying to head it off with his blunt nose.

When I picked it up Algy sat in front of me moving his feet impatiently, obviously wanting to play with the little creature, gazing upwards and drooling in a way which, if you did not know him, would make you think he was longing to eat it. Finally we put it in a box with wire netting over the top to keep the cats out; then Algy and I went to the river and brought back sand, and finally made the tiny tortoise a little rock garden with a pool and tiny pot plants and lots of stones to bask on. We chopped up a little piece of raw meat and put it in the pool, and the tortoise became very happy in its home. I never saw it eat, but I expect it got insects off the fresh greenery we gave it every day.

Algy would sit beside the box for hours, gazing at his treasure, or woofing at me to take it out so that it would run about as Algy leaped around and blew on it, which did not frighten the little thing in the very least. It grew very slowly, but finally it was big enough to have a small hole drilled in the edge of its shell, so that it could be tethered beneath a tank to browse on the growing plants. It used to bob its head out at Algy's button nose when it wanted to play, and then retire into its shell-house when it was bored with him.

Algy was older than Ben, my Australian terrier, who was the second of the three dogs who were my greatest friends. Algy was friendly with Ben's mother, Pam, long before Ben was born, looking more like a fat black mouse than a puppy. Algy peered into the basket at this little creature, then snorted so loudly that Pam jumped and growled, then finally he proceeded to settle down to adoring the naughty little pup, and to doing his best in his loving, clumsy way to look after it. Between Algy and me I am afraid that Benny became a spoilt little monster. He bullied Algy from the moment he began to stagger about on fat, bandy legs, his portly tummy barely clearing the ground, and his sharp milk teeth taking nips at Algy's unprotected areas.

As Ben grew out of puppyhood, Algy still seemed to need something helpless to care for, and he adopted a series of the queerest babies. One morning at breakfast he came in from the garden and put a tiny, hairless, baby mouse down beside my porridge plate. It was rather bewildered and wet, but quite unhurt. Algy's possum was one pet that I found for him, for it came to live in a tree outside the nursery window, where it slept most of the day, and then got very lively towards the evening. I put milk and honey on the window-ledge, and sat very quietly watching it running about the branches. After a long time Possy became so tame that I could pick it up. Algy was entranced with the possum, and once it got used to being blown on, and to seeing the big smile split Algy's face almost in half, it really did not mind him at all.

Then one day I discovered it had a baby in its pouch. I was thrilled, and while it sat nibbling at the treats I brought it, it allowed me to put my finger in its pouch very gently indeed, and to hook the baby out of it. It was almost more than Algy could bear not to be allowed to lick it.

Mother and baby possum spent a lot of time scrambling round the nursery and making possum faces at Algy. Then father possum moved into the tree, but he was wild and fierce, and I never tamed him. One day he fell into the slippery porcelain bath and could not get out again. He sat there making angry 'kaaaa kaka-ka' noises, so I made a sort of rope ladder out of bath towels and fastened it to the window. Then I went out and closed the door, so that father's dignity would be safe as he climbed up the towels to freedom. He probably went back to mother possum and told her I was a nasty, interfering little girl, and that it was all

It used to bob its head out at Algy's button nose.

my fault that he had fallen into the bath in the first place.

Then Algy adopted a baby fox. It was only about four inches long except for its busy tail, and what he stood from that imp of Satan! He never lost his temper with it, and always seemed disappointed when I put it to bed at night because it had to be shut up; foxes have so many enemies – and are themselves the enemy of so many. Finally the half-grown fox ran away and Algy mourned for a while, then, though he seemed to forget his wild baby, I think he went to the river bank sometimes on a moonlit night and played for a while with the nursling. I have often missed him from beside my bed when I have wakened at the quick, sharp yapping of a nearby fox.

One of his funniest adopted children was his duckling. Algy always followed me through the hen-houses, and the hens were quite used to him. He would inspect all the old ladies who were sitting, sniffing at them and prodding them with his blunt nose so that their feathered bloomers rose in the air off the clutch they were hatching. The hens were most indignant at his interference; naturally they considered their eggs were none of his business. They must often have wondered whose business they were anyhow, because these broody old girls used to find themselves with families of turkeys or ducks instead of chickens, and once a pelican, a most rare visitor, laid two eggs in a hen's nest, which unfortunately never hatched.

One evening we had gone the rounds and collected the eggs and returned to the house. Algy squatted in front of where I sat in a low chair, his eager eyes on me and the funniest expression on his face! He was drooling a little from his big, flapping chops, and I said:

'Algy! Whatever are you holding in your mouth?'

He gulped with excitement, and must nearly have

swallowed whatever it was, because he bent his head suddenly and it fell a few inches to the floor. It was an egg, and that eager look was guilt, for he knew that he must never touch an egg. The short drop broke it and inside the shell, its feathers wet and its little yellow bill cheeping with indignation, was a tiny duckling. It must have been ready to crack its own shell, for it was quite strong. Algy put his nose near to it and gave a tremendous, excited snort – the gust hit the duckling and blew it back on its tail. It lurched to its small webbed feet and complained like Donald Duck himself! From then on the duckling was considered Algy's pet, and no one dreamed of eating it.

Unlike most small animals, my guinea pigs never got over their fear of Algy, and he gazed at them shivering with nervousness of him, while *he* trembled with anxiety to take care of them. The guinea pigs lived in an old-fashioned hen coop, the sort that has four corners, a wired top, and rests flat on the ground, so that it can be moved to fresh grass every day. One day Algy managed to open the little door of the coop and to squeeze his big body inside. There he crouched, and I found the four corners stuffed with cowering guinea pigs, while Algy pressed his square mug into the corner and bestowed large wet kisses on the terrified animals, because his nose was so square he could not get nearer to them than the tip of his tongue. It was one thing to get *in* the coop, but another to get him *out*. In the excitement of tipping the cage up to release Algy, I lost half the guinea pig family.

Like most dogs Algy hated to be laughed at, and I always tried not to do it, but one day I just could not help myself. One sunny morning I found him in the garden gazing at a small, gay lizard that was running up and down the wooden edge of a flower bed. Algy was trying to creep up to it, puffing madly, while the lizard ignored him, peering about with bright eyes and making little darts at flies. When Algy could not bear it any longer he put his great paw down, softly, on the lizard's tail, when to his great astonishment the lizard scurried off leaving its tail under his paw. He never really recovered from the mystery of the whole thing, and he brought the tiny tail and put it in my lap, his face still expressing extreme wonderment.

Another day he came to me woofing and blowing as he did when he had something to show me. So I followed him to the wild, shrub-tangled end of the garden, where he began to sniff at a glass bottle. I picked it up and inside was a large frill-lizard, although the neck of the bottle was much too small for it to get out. We decided that the lizard must have crept into the bottle when it was tiny, and that it lay there gorging on the flies and insects that the bottle trapped, until it grew too big to get out. I have seen many ships in bottles, but only one lizard, and it raised its frill in the way that ship-bottle builders pull up the masts. We kept it for a day or two, then Lewis cut the neck off the bottle and released the lizard. It scuttled awkwardly away, and Algy watched it with the air of an elderly professor who had suddenly been confronted with a problem he cannot solve.

Life went on very busily for me with all my pets to be cared for as well as Algy's favourites. He must have been about two years old, and Ben only about a year, when we had the great adventure that was to give me the most beautiful, kingly, aloof dog I have ever known, the dog who saved my life at least twice. He was not bought, we did not breed him, I found him, and perhaps that helped to make him more my dog than any dog I have ever known before or since, and this is how it happened.

3. Ajax

Australia is a land of violent contrasts. Sometimes the country suffers from a drought, and sometimes from rolling floods that carry away animals and houses, fences and even people. If you look at a map of Australia you will see where a river makes part of the border-line between New South Wales and Queensland, and half-way along this the river takes a sudden hairpin bend. The river has many names; sometimes it's called the Severn, sometimes the Sovereign, and sometimes the Dumeresque. My home was right on a bend. Its name Gunyan was an aboriginal word for 'running water'. At times there was far too much running water, for the homestead stood with the river curving round it on two sides, and in a really great flood the water overflowed the banks and poured down on the house, like someone taking a diagonal short-cut across a street corner.

I only remember one such flood, and while it was frightening and terrible, drowning animals and causing thousands of pounds' worth of damage, I could not help finding it exciting, and it did give me the most wonderful dog I have ever known – my golden giant, Ajax.

It had been raining for weeks, both at my home and far up-river where the small streams poured their rain-fed waters into the main channel of the river, swelling it into a great, thundering mass of water that broke its banks and spread into a swiftly-running torrent seven miles wide. My father got news by telephone of the approaching flood, and so we had time to make preparations to leave the homestead and move to higher land.

When my father said we must get ready to move, the dogs and I were very excited. We were to take tents and to go up on to a hill about three miles from the homestead, where we would be above the water however much it should rise. First of all everything possible had to be put away, so we helped stack furniture up in the big loft, then the car was driven up a ramp on to a high verandah and chained there. It was no use to us then, because the water in the small gullies lying between us and the hill we were making for was already too deep to cross in the car.

We had to make our trek in buggies and sulkies and drays. Of course the station hands and their families were coming too, and everybody rushed about, loading drays, packing blankets and tents and food. My mother and Nessie, who was our housekeeper now that I was too big to have a nurse, packed tins of food and cut sandwiches, gathered together changes of shoes and clothes, and finally said they were ready. I'd packed most of my toys and staggered up to the loft with them, then I put the bridle on Buck, my bay pony, to lead him by, for I was going in the sulky with Lewis, who was a wonderful bushman, full of the sort of stories that children love to listen to. I was to lead Buck because Algy and Ben would not stay in the sulky without me, and Algy was afraid of water and would have to be carried over the streams, while Benny was really too small to follow if I rode Buck over the water-covered bush roads, full of rubbish and nasty deep pot-holes.

Finally we were ready, and the oddest-looking cavalcade you ever saw set off for the hilltop, which looked down on the muddy, rushing yellow torrent. Poor drowned animals floated and bobbed on the current; great trees, uprooted as the water softened their earth-bound roots and toppled them into the flood, turned and twisted and bumped into tangles of fence posts and torn wires, and jams of planks, where houses had been washed away and broken up in the fury of the waters, to be carried perhaps hundreds of miles down-stream before being stranded by the receding river.

We reached the hilltop and the men began setting up the tents. The dogs and I seemed to be in everyone's way, so we walked down the hill to the edge of the river. It was a frightening sight, with water as far as your eyes could see, and once a small wooden cottage, all in one piece, went skimming by, twisting and turning in the current. The dogs and I stayed for a long time at the edge of the water, watching it creep up on the stick my father had driven into the mud to test the rate the river was rising. Once we saw a huge gum tree, its twisted roots, still earth-filled, towering above the water, hurtling along, twisting and turning and bumping other trees and logs; and as the current swept it towards us I saw a long, evil head reared above the roots, like the carved figure on the prow of a ship. Thick coils twined about the roots, patterned as perfectly as if woven by a Persian carpet-maker, and I knew it was a very big carpet-snake, a constrictor of the python type that sometimes grows to fifteen feet and more in length. It is harmless, but a great eater of hens and their eggs, and I knew that somebody was going to have an unwelcome visitor when the water finally left the tree stranded. However, that might be after a trip of hundreds of miles.

The dogs and I would have been quite happy to sit for hours by the water and watch the strange flotsam that went rushing by, but suddenly I became aware that not all the movement was on the water – the land around me was simply alive with creatures that had come out of their haunts to find high land out of reach of the river. There were frogs and spiders, centipedes and scorpions lizards and snakes and goodness knows what else – all travelling up the hill towards our tents!

Algy and Ben were more fascinated than I was by all the creepy-crawlies, and barked madly at the frogs, trying to anticipate which way they would jump. That was all right, but I was afraid they might pounce on one of the more deadly creatures, so we went back up the hill. It wasn't much better up there, as the tents seemed to be carpeted with spiders already, as well as other oddities, but fortunately all these disturbed creatures seemed more interested in finding somewhere to hide than in rushing about or attacking animals. I felt that a great big dog like Algy should protect *me* from the creeping things, but he didn't like them himself: if he was having a doze and woke with one crawling over him, he would twitch his hide and whimper for me until I came along and knocked it off. Ben, who wasn't much bigger than a good-sized lizard himself, was much braver, and had to be restrained from snapping at scorpions and spiders, and those horrible, ghost-white centipedes that you never see until something like a flood has chased them from the rotten logs they live in, where apparently they never see the sun.

Most of the station livestock had been moved back into the hills several days before. Cattle are hopeless in floods; horses, even sheep will try to swim, but cattle simply stand there until the water rises high enough to lift them off their hooves, turns them over and drowns them. So all the cattle in the river paddocks had been moved to higher lands, and the Hereford stud had their stablemen with them, well out of the reach of flood waters.

We had a camp-fire supper, and I was sent to bed almost as soon as it was dark. Algy and Ben lay on saddle cloths on the end of my camp stretcher. The whole place was wet and smelly and I was afraid of the whispering, rustling things that crawled about me in the dark, so I let Algy and Ben creep up on my bed and lie beside me, which in the ordinary way was strictly forbidden.

In the morning the water had fallen a few inches, and the dogs and I set out to explore; the small, teeming life did not seem so bad in the sunlight. The ground was squashy with wet, but the sun shone down with a cheerful warmth. We had gone out of sight of the camp, and were walking about among a lot of felled trees that had been chopped down in the summer; I walked cautiously around these, because you could not tell what might be lurking on the other side if you jumped over them. I was just running round one when I heard a whining, scratching sound in it. I listened and heard it again, and so did the dogs, and Benny began to dig violently at one end of the log. I pulled him away, because I was afraid of what he might find in there; then I marked the log, called the dogs and we raced back to the camp to find Lewis.

Lewis brought an axe and began to chop carefully at the waterlogged bark. There was no sound from inside it, and I think Lewis thought that I had imagined the noise; then a chip of wood came away, and underneath it we could see a bright, golden gleam. Lewis made the opening wider, put in his hand and pulled out a long, yellow puppy, quite dead.

'Well, there you are,' Lewis said. 'I'm afraid we are too late, the little chap's dead.'

'Oh, Lewis, how awful! But how long has he been dead?'

'About a day – perhaps more, I should think.'

'You mean he hasn't just died this minute?'

'No, he's quite cold, he's been dead some time.'

'Then he can't be the one I heard!' I shouted excitedly. 'There must be another one in there!'

So Lewis began his careful chopping again, and sure enough another bright golden gleam appeared. He tore the soft wood away with his hands and my heart sank; there was no movement at all, apparently this little chap was as dead as his brother. Lewis put his hand in to lift the pup, and pulled it back saying:

'Ouch! He bit me, the little demon!'

'Oh, he's alive! He's alive!'

'He's alive all right, and he's got a mighty fine set of milk teeth!'

Lewis put his hand back in the log more cautiously and lifted out another yellow pup, so nearly dead that it made little difference, but still with enough spirit to draw back his tiny upper lip and snarl at the big man holding him. Lewis handed him to me, saying:

'Here you are – I don't think he'll live, he seems all in, so you mustn't be upset if you lose him. Take him back to camp and get some warm milk and brandy from your mother – and wrap him up warmly.'

The dogs were leaping up like mad things, each trying to look at the pup, sniffing and yelping until I had to scold them and make them keep down. Once the little fellow made a feeble snap at my hand; his teeth closed on the skin, but he hadn't enough strength in his jaws to break it. After that he seemed to lose consciousness, and his yellow head, small and babyish yet somehow full of character, lolled against my arm, and his yellow eyes stayed closed.

I walked back as quickly as I could and wrapped the baby in an old jersey, warmed some milk and added a few drops of brandy and forced it between his jaws. He swallowed a little and I lay down on my bed, holding him close to me for warmth and making the dogs stay at the foot, which annoyed them very much. All that day I fed the pup on milk and brandy every hour. If he wasn't any stronger he certainly hadn't lost strength, and then I fed him every two hours all through the night. My mother wanted to help me, but I wanted to care for him all myself, so she let me. The next morning the pup was brighter, and I was half dead with sleepiness! Once he tried to struggle up, and snarled and gave quite a brisk snap at my hand. I left him asleep on my bed when I went to get my breakfast, and rushed into the tent again when I heard a violent yelp from Benny. I discovered that Master Ben, taking advantage of my absence, had been nosing around the pup, and had his black button of a nose well nipped for his pains!

That afternoon I was very sleepy, so after I had fed the pup I lay down beside him, and went off to sleep. I must have slept very soundly, for when I woke the pup was not there, and the jumper I had rolled round him trailed from the bed to the ground. I jumped up and hurried to the tent-flap, pushed it aside, and there I saw a sight I shall never forget.

Outside on the wet ground I saw a circle of dogs. In it were Algy, and Ben, and the sheep and cattle dogs belonging to the stockmen. In the centre of the ring stood my tiny, savage, golden pup. He swayed on his legs, but a faint, ominous growl came from the small golden chest – as he grew older this faint ghost of a growl turned into the deep, shuddering thunder of the fighter – his lips were drawn back, and his brilliant yellow eyes were filled with flickering pink lightnings. This wee, starved pup was defying a dozen full-grown dogs in his lonely, friendless world! My heart went out to him as I watched; his hind legs gave way and he sat down, but he still kept his head high and rumbled his tiny defiance of the crowd.

I couldn't bear it any longer, he was so alone. I stepped forward and picked him up. His sharp eye-teeth broke the skin on my hand and drops of blood welled out. I left my hand in his jaws, and he looked up at me uncertainly; I stroked his head with my other hand, and he opened his jaws. I kept on stroking him and presently he licked the salty blood off my hand with a wondering expression.

Then I held him against my face and whispered to him: 'Do you know that you're *my* dog – that you're Ajax, my god of the lightning?'

He licked my cheek and that ended our first battle of wills. I had won, he was my dog, my Ajax – for ever.

4. Ajax Rescues Me

Once the flood began to go down, the river and the little creeks that fed it dropped rapidly. Actually I had only had Ajax for two days when my father decided that it would be safe to begin the trek home. So we packed up everything once again, and started off home; I holding Ajax on my knee, and the other two dogs sitting jealously, Algy at my feet, Benny on the seat between Lewis and me. It wasn't at all a pleasant drive. There were only patches of dry road, and all sorts of things were hidden in the watery holes and pools, logs and washed away earth; I had my work cut out trying to hold on to all three dogs as we went bumping along.

When we reached the homestead we found it in a horrible mess of mud and rubbish, but safe. An appalling smell hung over everything; the river had risen to nearly two feet high in the house and the floors were a foot deep in smelly mud and dead crawlies – and not all of them were dead either! Everyone worked at shovelling the mud out until hoses could be put on. Finally it was pretty clean, but it stayed damp and beastly for days, and as for the garden, it was absolutely ruined. In the end the river mud did it a lot of good, the way that the overflowing Nile feeds the crops, but nearly everything had to be replanted.

Ajax grew stronger every day, and soon he could lap up his milk; then his yellow eyes would narrow to slits of ecstasy as he drank. When he got a little larger and stronger on his legs, Algy longed to play with him. He would bowl the pup over and push him along with his nose, while Ajax went on with frenzied snappings and snarlings. Then Algy blinked at the ridiculous pup, seemed to shrug his big shoulders, and probably gave up the effort. When Ajax snapped at Benny, Benny snapped back at him, and then there were such squealings and yelpings of rage on both sides that I had to separate them.

Ajax grew into a tremendous dog. He never played with other dogs and he just tolerated humans. He seemed to get the exercise his huge frame needed on long, nightly hunting trips from which he would return and throw himself down beside my bed until morning. I was the one thing he loved, and he hardly took his deep yellow eyes off me. I hated to go anywhere without him, for when I went away he was filled with savage despair. In a couple of years he grew nearly as big as a calf, and his coat was a glorious orange-golden colour. We decided that his mother must have been a dingo, those clever, savage Australian wild dogs, and his father, most likely, was a big kangaroo dog. Kangaroo dogs are like giant greyhounds, very fast on their feet, with great deep chests, and bony, intelligent heads.

When Ajax was three, my family took a house at the seaside for the summer. I was excited about this, but miserable at the thought of leaving the dogs behind, especially Ajax who would be so unhappy without me. Nevertheless I had to go. When we arrived at a quiet cove below Sydney called Half-Moon Bay, I was delighted with the bungalow, which was built high above the ground, with a sort of open-air playroom beneath with a table-tennis table and other joys, and all around it a big, high-fenced garden. The wire-netting fence was there to keep away marauding dogs. The house overlooked the beach and the splendid, wild waters of the Pacific, with waves like emerald galleons topped by wind-torn white sails.

The morning after we arrived, after spending nearly a week in Sydney on the way down, I was plunging about in the surf when a 'dumper' – that's a big wave full of churning undertow – caught me, knocked me down, and then landed me on the beach in a smother of sand and water. When I got my breath and opened my eyes, I was knocked down again – by Algy and Ben! They scrabbled and yelped and smothered me. Algy, in moments of excitement, always imagined he was a tiny puppy again and wanted to sit on my knee, so there he was, knocking me down and trying to sit on me at the same time!

When I managed to look up, Lewis was standing behind me, his dark face creased with laughter. I called out:

'Oh, Lewis, how lovely – where's Ajax?'

'He's waiting in the garden. I didn't know how he'd take to the beach if there was a crowd here, I didn't realize it would be so quiet –'

'But how did you get here?'

'Well, I think you have to thank Ajax. I had an awful job with him after you left. He kept starting out to find you. So I wired to your father after a day of this, and got my orders to drive the truck down and bring all the boys along – we've covered about five hundred miles in the last four days – look!'

He broke off and pointed to where, against the skyline on the edge of the sand, stood a colossal, orange-coloured dog. The dog stood motionless for a second, and then I called 'Ajax!' and he left the bank; he didn't seem to jump, he just launched himself into space, and the next instant I was knocked flat and Ajax stood over me, his feet planted on each side of my body, his serious, savage eyes gazing into mine. The wild light died out of them, and I put my hand up to his muzzle. He gave a little whine, strange from such a great, gaunt creature, and I think the only whine I ever heard him give; then he put his head down and licked my face. I put my arms round his neck and pulled myself up, then we all went home to breakfast.

Each of the dogs had a different approach to the surf that curled and hissed up the long crescent of coarse, golden sand. Benny rushed at it, biting the bubbles and wobbling ludicrously behind as he backed away from a wave, and he always thought the waves were chasing him up the beach. Algy mumbled in his chops, then put his head on one side until his expression said quite plainly:

'Somebody's fooling me! And I *won't* go in that great big bath!' Finally he licked at the froth, paddled a little where the sand was wet from the spent waves, decided that it was quite harmless after all, and settled down to enjoy himself. The small crabs fascinated him, he sniffed at them, then leapt back wildly as they nipped his nose! His chops flapped with slapping sounds that startled the crabs, and always made me laugh.

Ajax looked neither to right nor left. He followed me a few steps into a rushing wave, breasted it with me, and calmly followed into the deep water and swam beside me as if he had done it all his life. I think that Ajax really loved the water apart from his wish to stay near to me. He was a very strong swimmer, and would tow me along whenever I put my hand on his neck. Sometimes he let me swim by myself, but he always lay on the sand and watched until I came out again.

One fine morning I woke early and decided to go for a swim. Ajax was off on one of his prowls, and I could hear Ben and Algy quarrelling about something at the back of the house, so I decided to trick them and slip off alone. The sun was still below the horizon, but it made a track of light from the beach to the end of the sea-filled world. It was high tide and the sea looked oily and heavy, with no waves to speak of. I decided that there was probably a heavy undertow and that I must be careful. I kicked off my sandals and waded in. The sudden, crisp, cool shock of the water was wonderful, and I began swimming.

Presently I thought I was far enough from the shore and turned to swim in, but I couldn't. I could feel the strong grip of the water drawing me away from the beach. I knew I mustn't panic. I let myself float for a moment to regain my strength, and was alarmed to find that I was being carried seawards even more swiftly than I thought. I was very afraid; I couldn't fight the undertow, and the sea was so deep and undisturbed that it was likely to attract the deadly Grey Nurse sharks. It was a nasty thought that those powerful, hungry fish might be cruising near to me quite unseen. I grew more and more afraid; I tried to control myself, but as the weakness of weariness crept over me the terror mounted. I turned my head towards the shore and called despairingly:

'Ajax! Ajax!'

It seemed minutes afterwards, but it could only have been seconds, when I heard feet thudding on the beach. I turned my head, and bounding across the pale gold of the early-morning sands was the darker golden shape of Ajax. He sprang from the hard-packed sand at the edge of the water like something launched from a catapult, and then I could see his great head moving strongly towards me across the terrifying waste of water. In a minute or so the head came nearer to me, and as I put my arm across his neck he turned towards the shore, and I saw my father and Lewis there. They were struggling to launch the little boat we kept dragged up on the dry sand, out of reach of the tide.

Even Ajax, strong swimmer though he was, could make no headway against the terrible pull of the undertow; he could barely hold his own with my added weight dragging at him. I was too exhausted to help, and could only hang on and try not to hamper the dog too much. I thought I could hear my father's voice shouting encouragement, but I felt that even Ajax's great strength was waning. His shoulders moved more slowly, though his gallant heart kept him trying.

I don't remember much more, although I became conscious that the boat was beside me, and I had only one idea fixed firmly in my mind, I must not let go of Ajax. My father told me afterwards that they just could not pry my hands loose from Ajax's neck, and that they had to pull the great dog and me into the boat in one piece. At one stage they decided to tow us in, but they, too, thought of the sharks, so with a great struggle they finally hauled the dog in with me attached.

When we reached the beach my father rolled me in his coat, made a sand-pillow for my head, and told me to lie there quietly. For once in his life Ajax lost his aloofness. No human face could have expressed greater anxiety for a loved one; he padded softly round me, every now and again putting his big head down close to mine, licking my hand, and finally lying close beside me.

In a few minutes I felt better, then my father told me that he and Lewis decided on an early morning swim too, and as they were leaving the house they heard a rush of feet and saw Ajax tear down the garden and sail over the fence. They decided that this must mean that I was in some sort of danger, and they ran after the dog. When they reached the beach they

I called despairingly, 'Ajax! Ajax!'

could see Ajax's head far out in the path of sunlight, and beyond it a small dot that they knew must be mine. They tore for the boat, and it was then that Ajax reached me and I saw them over his head.

The rest of the holiday was heavenly. Benny, especially, was fascinated by the life in the deep pot-holes studding the rocks. These holes were round and quite deep, for they are ground out by the tides swirling stones round and round in the same places for years until the holes are formed, and finally these become the homes of all sorts of sea creatures. Crabs were always fascinating mysteries to Ben as well as to Algy. He would poke his nose into thick bunches of seaweed, give a surprised yell as something nipped him, and back away. Then he would creep back cautiously, unable to control his curiosity, and then retire again with a shriek of surprise and a backward bound, and sometimes he would have a small, outraged crab fastened to his sharp nose! Then Benny would squint down it, fill his lungs for a colossal yelp – and as likely as not the crab would drop off! At that, Benny staggered back on his haunches, looking for the back, or non-nipping end of this strange creature – and the crab scuttled off sideways!

Oh, it was fun – and even Ajax showed amazement at one friend I made. I was gazing into a tiny rock pool, when I noticed what I took to be a piece of strange, speckled seaweed. I touched it gently with my finger and it curled over the tip – I was holding hands with a baby octopus! I peered into the pool and could see its eight little arms waving about in the water, each one just a few inches long. Its queer little face seemed merely a pair of eyes and a strange sort of tiny beak. I put my hand into the water and managed to detach it gently from its rock. It wound its tentacles round my hand. The dogs were wild with excitement, each wanting to look, and I laughed when the dignified Ajax jerked his head away in a far from dignified manner when the baby touched his nose!

Algy was affectionate, as he was to all small creatures, and Benny belligerent, and he had to be scolded and kept in his place. The little octopus wasn't at all frightened, merely active; he untwined himself from my hand and ran up my arm and over my shoulder, perched there a minute and then ran down my back and dropped on to the rocks. Once on the rock he drew himself up high on his eight arms and bustled back into the pool, just like a Walt Disney octopus.

Those lazy, sun-filled days were full of unusual excitements for an inland-bred child, for even the finding of an old plank, washed up in the tide and covered with goose-necked barnacles, was thrilling. The dogs were madly excited over the barnacle-covered plank, and barked and bounded about it as the myriad heads waved about in their aimless manner, like the result of a badly-done 'perm'. I think the plank looked to the boys like one long and very peculiar animal!

The summer ended at last, and as our return road home meant going through Sydney we stayed a few days for my mother to do some shopping. It was not easy to manage the dogs in a town, for none of them had ever worn collars, and they had not a clue about traffic; so it meant that nearly all their exercise, in fact their whole life, was lived on the roof of the hotel. My family had always stayed in this particular hotel and they were very good about the dogs, so it really was not too difficult as it was only for a few days anyhow.

It was during this stay that we all acquired a new friend, so it was worth a little inconvenience.

5. Kiko

In the few days we stayed at the 'Metropole' with the dogs, my mother was busy interviewing possible governesses for me. I did not think much of this idea as I had never had regular lessons, but as I could read and write quite well by the time I was five I hated the idea of having to learn anything else! My father and I would spend hours at the Zoo, Taronga Park, and as I loved the monkeys I used to get the keepers to let me follow them into the various cages so that I could nurse the gibbons, give the chimpanzees their milk, and take the orang-utans for walks.

It was while I was doing this that I made a wonderful friend, an old sea captain who loved monkeys too. He used to bring consignments of animals from the East for the Australian zoos, and when I met him he was visiting the last batch of monkeys he had brought. Usually these little tropical monkeys die on the voyage down, because the nights on sea are cold for monkeys born in the steamy, tropical forests of Malaya. The Captain hated to see the poor little beasts huddled together and very miserable, for monkeys get sea-sick, and they develop pneumonia very easily.

So as soon as his ship put to sea, the Captain made all his sailors sew little pyjamas for the monkeys. The tough sailors were digusted at being turned into monkeys' tailors, but the Captain insisted; and then when the pyjamas were finished the sailors had to catch the monkeys every evening and put them on, and then undress them every morning! The monkeys bit and scratched, but every evening the Captain inspected the forty little monkeys in forty little suits of pyjamas, and said good night to them. As a result of this care none of the monkeys died – but the sailors were very glad when the voyage was over.

The Captain came to lunch at the hotel with us one day. Afterwards I took him up to meet the dogs, and even the aloof Ajax could not help liking him. Then he and I went off to walk round the town. As we came out of the hotel we heard the sound of rollicking music in the street, and saw a young Italian turning the handle of a barrel organ. On it was the smallest, most miserable monkey. It had a belt and heavy chain round its waist, and it wore a wisp of a dirty red coat and a silly cap above its pinched little face. It was shivering with cold, for it was May, and May in Sydney can be very cold indeed. The Captain gave me a penny to give the little monkey, and it put out its little paw and ignored the penny, just clinging to my finger.

The Italian went on turning his hurdy-gurdy, and I lifted the monkey in my arms and it pressed its shivering body against me for warmth while it cheeped softly in the saddest way. It was one of the many varieties of capuchin monkey, the Captain said, but it looked like a squirrel with its long tail which should have been fluffy, but which was very motheaten-looking. Most of the monkeys on barrel organs have rather wiry fur with a greenish tinge, and stand upright, and have tails like whips. This one was small and soft and very miserable.

I was nearly in tears when I put the little thing on the top of the organ and it tried to creep back to me again. The Captain gave the boy some money and told him to buy the monkey a warmer coat, and we walked on.

We heard a voice calling us, and found the Italian walking towards us, while in the distance the monkey crouched, trying to huddle itself together against the cold wind. The man wanted the Captain to buy the monkey, but the Captain refused. The Italian persisted, so I walked back and picked the monkey up again, and stood sheltering it from the cold wind.

Presently both men came back; the man spoke to me, smiling so that his teeth shone in the sunlight, but I did not care, I only wanted to keep the monkey warm. He unfastened the heavy chain and put the end in my hand.

'You taka da monk,' he said, still grinning. I looked towards the Captain, who was smiling.

'It's your monkey now,' he said.

'But doesn't he want it any more?'

'He's going away –'

'The gentlman, he buya da monk,' the man explained.

'Oh! Is it for *me* – do you really mean it belongs to me?' I was too excited to believe it.

'It does – if your mother'll let you have it.'

'Oh, thank you!' I said, 'I do love it!'

I pulled my coat round the little monkey and we went back to the hotel and found my mother writing letters. She was rather horrified at my cuddling such a dirty little thing in its horrible rag of a coat, but I could see how upset she was at its neglected condition. She went upstairs and put on her hat and brought down a warm scarf to wrap around the little monkey, then we got in a cab and set off for the vet's.

The vet said there was nothing wrong with my monkey except neglect; he took off the belt and chain and found its middle sore and raw, so he took the little thing away, and in about a quarter of an hour he returned with a much cleaner monkey, bandaged round the tum. We bought a light belt and chain, and then some grapes and bananas, and as we could not buy a coat for the monkey we bought some soft flannel, and my mother said she would make one.

Then we went back to the hotel, wondering how we would smuggle the little fellow in, and pretty sure that the housemaid who did our rooms would not give us away! My father came in and said that finding a monkey did not surprise him, he always expected to find one new pet whenever he came back. The Captain named my new pet Kiko, and we bought it a basket for a bed, so that I could carry him about, on to the roof, and into the parks.

I knew the dogs would not hurt him, although Master Ben, who was used to being the smallest pet, could be quite cross if I made a fuss over an even smaller gentleman; and I certainly wondered how Kiko would take to them! I was due for a big surprise, although I was right about Benny; he was a little jealous. Algy loved Kiko at once, but Ajax, who was so indifferent, was as nearly affectionate to Kiko as it was possible for him to be. It was to Ajax that Kiko always went whenever he was with the three dogs, and Ajax liked it. He would stretch out in the sunlight, pretending to doze and looking quite beautiful with his orange coat giving back the sunlight, and Kiko would creep between his big forelegs, right up under his chin, while Ajax nuzzled him as he never did any other creature.

We all enjoyed the long trip home, although I did not want to leave the Captain, and Kiko soon lost his sore middle and climbed about the car, slept on my lap, or played with the dogs quite happily, through the long days of motoring over about five hundred miles of bad roads.

When we reached home Kiko took up residence in my nursery. He seldom climbed like other monkeys, but he would run about the floor with his bushy tail down between his hind legs and curling up in front of his chest like a tiny sleigh with a scroll-like prow. When he wore his belt and chain and it got in the way, he picked the chain up in one velvet-soft paw and lifted it around, as a lady might lift a train.

Kiko soon grew a beautiful, silky coat, and he would croon and cheep happily to himself all day long. He loved being made much of, and developed an enormous appetite for such a tiny creature. He had very nice table manners, and would take a grape gently from your palm, patting it with his other paw as if to say thank you. I believe he had a happy life. He was a busy little fellow and had his own toy-box. At night I would put his toys away, in the morning he would take them out again. His favourite toy was a scrap of carpet, which he would tack down with drawing-pins, hammered in with a little hammer taken from my brother's tool-chest. At night I would pull it up. In the morning he would start afresh; he never got tired of it and he never hit his thumb! When he got tired of playing, Ajax would lie down while Kiko crept over him until *he* got tired; then they both went to sleep.

As no suitable governess had turned up for me I had a reprieve. I always knew that eventually I would have to go to boarding school, and I hated the idea, but fifteen still seemed an awfully long way away. So I went on happily enjoying my dogs and Kiko, and looking forward to the Show, which that year was to be combined with a circus and many sideshows, and was due a few weeks after we arrived home.

6. We Claim Waltzing Matilda

Most bush excitements are connected in some way with horses. In Australia you do not learn to ride, you just *do*, and you begin when you are so young that there seems there never was a time when you did not ride. English riding is much more stylized than Australian. In England you learn how to sit and how to hold your hands and feet, and what to do if your horse makes an unexpected move. The saddles, too, in England are less flat and slippery than Australian saddles, and the stirrup-leathers are shorter. Australians ride by balance and instinct, keeping their hands low because it seems the most effective way in which to cope with a horse's mouth. The horses seldom trot, but break straight from a walk to a canter, and for long distances they go at a rather horrible jog.

We never rode for enjoyment, except in shows. Riding was simply a method of working and getting from one place to another, and the stockmen simply could not understand it at all when our English friends used to want to 'go for a ride'!

A professional stockbreaker came around the station at least once a year. In the middle of the cattle yards there is always a round yard with a tall, strong fence, for it is in this yard that the breaker rides his wild horses.

Of course I adored this, and used to sit on the top rail so as to have a front seat, holding Ben beside me, while Algy and Ajax stayed below. Then the breaker sprang on to the wild horses, and rode them bucking and snorting around the yard, in a whirl of dust and sweat, until the poor beasts, broken indeed, came trembling to a standstill. It was a cruel method, but with so many horses to break in, and so few men to do it, it could not be helped. Of course thoroughbred horses got a much better deal and a slower breaking-in, but with the mass of half-wild horses brought from the far paddocks, and not very different from the wild horses which are called 'brumbies', these hard, rapid methods made them rideable, but never really tame or pleasant to ride.

Every year, too, the foals were brought in for branding, and what a mob of wild, leggy little creatures they were. Sometimes one of the stockmen would put a rope halter on a foal and hoist me up on to its back. Then when it bucked madly, and I shot into the air, one of the other men would catch me! I loved this, and of course it was quite safe with the men looking after me, and it went on until I got too heavy to catch.

Naturally, with horses playing such a big part in everyone's life, any entertainment like a buck-jumping show had to be very good indeed. One of these shows was more famous than any of the others, for the star horse was considered the savagest buckjumper in the country, and the man who rode him an unbeatable rider. So when it got around that this man, Billy Weight, and his horse Bobs were coming to the Show we looked forward to it very much indeed. There were to be other sideshows and the inevitable merry-go-round. Strange to think that bush children who rode so many real horses were so excited about climbing on to little wooden horses, and being whirled round and round to the hurdy-gurdy music of the calliope! Of course you have to remember that most bush children had not seen a train, or even a tall building, or the sea, and these little shows held all the glamour and excitement of the year for them.

When this particular show opened my father and I drove to it in a car that was rather like one of today's shooting brakes, but we just called it the truck. The sides were netted in, so that the dogs could ride in there, and we took them nearly anywhere with us. They hated staying at home, and in the truck they would simply lie down and sleep when we left them.

When we reached the show my father and I started around the sideshows, leaving the dogs in the truck. We laughed at ourselves and each other in the distorting mirrors, and I had a ride on the merry-go-round. We called on an old friend, the snake-handler, who was wading about the snake pit in a pair of pink knitted bootees, through which, he claimed, the snakes could not get their fangs.

Then it was time for the buckjumping show, and it seemed that the tent held every bushman for miles around, because in a country of fine riders Billy Weight was considered the finest of them all. He was a half-caste (these men are often wonderful riders) and Bobs his horse, was unique. Real buckjumpers are very rare. Lots of horses buck in a way, but it is mostly what is called pigrooting, they put their heads down, arch their backs and jump along in a stiff-legged way. This is fairly hard to sit, but the *real* buckjumper is almost unrideable, for it gives a sort of twist to its body in mid-air, all four feet off the ground. Bobs was the real thing, and some of the finest riders in Australia could not sit him.

Inside the buckjumping tent, the ring was quite a small one of trodden-down earth, surrounded by a strong rail fence to keep the bucking horses from breaking through – this sometimes happened anyhow! The tent was lit by smoke flares. There were no seats, everybody stood, and the tent was packed with tough, leathery bushmen waiting to see this rider who was supposed to be better than themselves. Most of the crowd knew my father, and they let me wriggle through their legs until I was beside the ring; then one man lifted me up and perched me on his shoulder.

In films of American rodeos, the horses are saddled and mounted in a horse-sized yard we called a 'crush', so that they cannot plunge about; but that is not the way we do it in Australia. There the saddle may be put on in the crush, and it is a slippery 'poly' saddle without knee-pads, something like a large racing saddle; then the gate of the crush is opened, the horse dashes out, and is mounted free in the ring.

From where I was perched on a tall bushman's shoulder I saw Bobs come charging into the ring. He was a great bay, eighteen hands high, glistening with sweat and fury. Then Billy Weight slipped into the ring. He was a small man, lithe as a cat, an old felt hat in one hand, and soft-soled sneakers on his feet. Bobs reared and plunged, and when he was ready Billy ran a few steps across the ring and sprang high on that twisting, rolling demon's body. He shouted, and hit the horse with his old hat, and the intensity and savagery of the horse's tremendous twisting leaps were thrilling to watch. The bushmen around me *knew* how great a rider this man was.

When Billy thought Bobs had had enough he slipped to the ground, the gates opened, and Bobs charged out again. It was as though a bolt of lightning had left the ring; once again it was just a dimly-lit, earth-floored circle.

After that we left the buckjumping tent and noticed one announcing 'Boxing Kangaroo'. My father was not very keen on this, he did not like kangaroos being made to box; but I was very insistent, so he let me go

He sprang high on that twisting, rolling demon's body.

in. There were not many people in the tent, and on one side of the little roped-in ring was a biggish lavender kangaroo. It stood dejectedly there, and its coat was dull and patchy in the dim light, so I walked along and rubbed its ears. It pressed its head against my hand, and I thought how gentle the big animal was.

Then the showman made some sort of speech to which I did not listen. A man stepped into the ring and the showman tied boxing gloves on to his hands. Then he came over to where I was with the kangaroo, and began to put another pair of gloves on to the animal, which pulled away and seemed frightened. The man growled at it and held on roughly. I said:

'It doesn't want those things on its hands, why don't you leave it alone?'

The man laughed unpleasantly:

'If she don't fight I lose me money. Come on you –' and he pushed the kangaroo into the middle of the ring. The kangaroo's arms looked so thin and its little paws were lost inside the big gloves, but the showman pushed it in front of the man it was to fight. It balanced on its tail, and the man hit it on the side of the head. The poor thing moved back, the showman shouted, and the man slapped it again as it moved backwards in clumsy, frightened hops. My father took my arm and said:

'You must come away; you don't want to watch this.'

Suddenly I was furious with the people standing around who did want to watch this poor creature, and I could not stand it. I pulled away from my father and ducked under the railing into the ring, and ran between the kangaroo and the man, shouting:

'You leave her alone, you big bully!'

The man laughed and so did the crowd. I was terribly angry and went on shouting.

'You wouldn't laugh if Ajax and Algy were here – Ajax! Algy! Here! Here, boys!'

My father stood by the ring, watching that I did not get myself into real trouble. He hated cruelty too, but as I was always rushing into things he decided that I must learn not to begin anything I could not finish by myself.

The showman tried to pull me away from the kangaroo, but I shut my eyes and hung on, shouting for the dogs. How the dogs got out of the truck I will never know, but suddenly the crowd in the tent parted and Ajax reached me in one bound over the low railings. His eyes flickered with red fire, and the deep, shuddering thunder in his chest sent the showman scurrying back from me.

Then Algy galumphed into the ring, panting and growling, followed by Benny, who was yapping his head off and making more noise than the other two put together, although he was so tiny.

The showman and the boxer backed out of the ring and looked nervously at the dogs. My father just watched. He knew that Ajax would not move unless someone touched me – and no one was likely to do that while the great dog stood beside me, still as a statue except for the deep breaths rumbling in his chest. Algy stood squarely on the other side of me, great head down, snorting and rumbling, and Ben danced around in a frenzy of excitement, not in the least knowing what it was all about.

'Don't you dare touch my kangaroo!' I shouted at the showman; and the man shouted back:

'*Your* kangaroo! I like that! I'll show yer –' He took a step towards me – and Ajax took a step towards *him*. He moved back hastily.

'Hi, mister!' he called to my father, 'call yer dawgs off will yer – yer little girl's spoilin' my show –'

My father said: 'Better my little girl than the police. You know well enough what you'd get if anyone reported the condition of that kangaroo: there'd be no show at all.'

Then someone in the crowd shouted:

'We've paid our money!'

'I don't care – no one's going to hurt my kangaroo!' I shouted back, and then the crowd began to laugh, and we must have looked very funny, the three dogs, the kangaroo and I, all bunched together in the centre of the ring, and the angry showman not daring to come near us. I began taking the gloves off the kangaroo while Ajax and Algy kept guard.

The whole thing ended by my father buying the kangaroo. Then the crowd moved back to let us pass, and we, accompanied by the kangaroo, all walked out to the cheers of the crowd. When we got outside my father said to me:

'You know, these wars you get yourself into are very expensive for me.'

'Oh, I know, Daddy – but we couldn't leave the poor thing.'

'What would you have done if the dogs hadn't been able to get to you, and if the owner hadn't agreed to sell – and if I hadn't been there to buy it for you?'

Well, there were no answers to that, so as the kangaroo did not seem at all afraid of the dogs we put her in the back of the truck and christened her Matilda.

Algy adored her; he was sure he had saved her, and she became his own special thing. Ajax did not care about anything as long as I was safe, and as for Benny – he might have bought Matilda with his own money, from his air of personal triumph.

Matilda made friends with everyone, and soon grew fat and sleek, nibbling about the garden and playing games with Algy, which she always ended by prodding him with the long toe on her hind foot. Algy spent happy hours lying in the shade while Matilda moved about him, nibbling grass blades; in fact the whole thing proved to be a beautiful friendship which began when Algy, like a brave knight of old, rescued a beautiful maiden. And she *was* beautiful, with soft eyes and small, helpless hands – and a very long and very muscular tail!

7. Circumstantial Evidence

You might think that with Kiko in possession of my nursery, and Matilda hopping about the garden, that winter would have been an enjoyable one. But it began with my grandmother getting ill and my mother going off to look after her, and then it went on to bring me great sorrow over Ajax.

In the bush the greatest crime a man can commit is to steal stock, and the very worst thing any dog can do is to kill stock. That is why the Australian wild dogs, dingoes, are destroyed so relentlessly, for they are the worst of all killers. They kill because it amuses them, and on a moonlight night one dingo might kill several hundred sheep, ripping them up the belly and leaving the poor brutes to die.

Because my home was a cattle station, dingoes were not quite such a menace to us, and probably we did not go to quite such lengths to destroy them as the sheepmen did. That is why I so often heard their mournful howling, as I lay in bed on moonlit nights. Dingoes are very clever, some bushmen say that they can count up to five or six; and sometimes one man will camp out in the bush, all alone, with nothing else to do but try and destroy probably *one* dingo.

The cows of our dairy herd, which supplied the milk for the station, were always separated from their calves at night, so that they would have plenty of milk in the morning. The calves were penned into the milking yard, and the cows grazed about outside.

One morning the milkman had risen early as he always did. It was a crisp winter morning, and when he reached the yard he was surprised to see the calves huddling together in one corner, instead of frisking about as usual. They were calling loudly for their mothers. On the ground at the side of the yard farthest from the calves were four others, four little bundles of red and white hide, and in the muddy ground around them was the imprint of huge paws. Outside the fence the mothers pressed against the rails and mooed unhappily.

Frank, the milkman, came straight back to tell my father. I heard them talking, and we waited for Lewis while Frank called him, then we all started for the yard together. My father wanted me to stay behind, but I would not; in my heart I was terribly afraid, and I had to go and look for myself.

The railings round the yard were of old, rotted wood, and the killer dog had leaped the top rail instead of crawling underneath, as most domesticated dogs would have done. Although the killing looked like the work of a dingo, Lewis thought that there was one very strange thing about it; dingoes kill sheep, they don't kill calves unless they are very hungry, and this one hadn't been hungry, for the calves were untouched except for the one savage slash which is the dingo's trademark when he kills for the sole joy of killing. And besides, he must have run right past a mob of sheep which were kept for mutton, and were grazing in the same paddock as the milking cows.

There were paw marks in the soft ground near the fence, and a white mark on the top rail, where a bit of bark had been ripped off when the dingo leaped over, and landed on the soft ground inside the yard. The rest of the marks were from the terror-stricken rushing about of the calves, a confusion of prints, sharp little hoofmarks and heavy pad marks. We all stood silently looking down at one big, clear, paw mark. Then Frank spoke slowly, with a worried look at me.

'I never seen a dingo with paws *that* big – it looks like . . .' he hesitated a moment.

'Like what, Frank?' my father asked.

'I don't like to say it, boss, but there's only one dog about here big enough to make them marks –'

My father glanced at me, I couldn't speak. Ajax stood beside me, a great, golden statue of a dog, with proud, aloof eyes.

'No! Not Ajax!' I said, and put my hand on the big head. Ajax moved against me and his throat rumbled, as if he thought that I was being menaced.

'He's a mighty queer dog, miss,' Frank said apologetically. 'I never seen one like him in all my life –'

'He's a mighty fine dog too,' my father broke in, 'and we can't condemn him on this sort of evidence. Frank, I think you'd better clear up this mess while we think what's best to do – and you come with me,' he added, looking at me. Ajax and I followed my father. I couldn't speak, I was cold with fear and misery.

'Ajax is a strange dog as Frank said,' my father put his hand on my shoulder, 'and if he's turned killer you know that there is only one thing – a bullet. *You* know that, and that if we don't shoot him someone else will, when this gets about. It would be better for Ajax to be killed painlessly by someone who loved him, than to be shot at by some stranger, and perhaps only wounded.'

Still I couldn't speak. I knew that my father was right. After a while I managed to mumble:

'Not yet! Not yet *please*! You don't *know* that Ajax did it! You can't hurt him, he saved my life!'

'No, we don't know that he did it, but it looks bad for him. I promise you that we'll be quite sure before we do anything. We owe Ajax a very big debt for what he did for you, and you know that I won't forget that – I only wish your mother wasn't away, but I don't want her to hurry back if we can help it,' he added in a worried voice.

I was very unhappy, for I knew something that my father did not know; I knew that Ajax, who was generally so quiet beside my bed, had been restless for the last two nights, and that last night when I sat up to see what was the matter with my dog I found him standing like a statue beside my bed. I put my hand under his muzzle to rub it and I felt something sticky. When I looked there was blood on my hand. I thought then that Ajax must have been hunting as he often did, just that; it was not until the morning that I learned, in terror and misery, what this hunting might have meant.

As I always did when I was in difficulties, I went to Lewis and we talked it over, but I did not tell even Lewis about the blood on Ajax's jaws the night before. Talking didn't help at all. We both knew that it boiled down to the question of whether Ajax was guilty or innocent. If he was guilty, he must die. The only alternative was to keep him tied up for life, and we both knew that was unthinkable; it would only inflict a slow death on the proud, fighting spirit.

I walked down to the river's edge, and sat for a long time with my arms round my dog's neck, and I knew that he was trying to comfort me with his nearness. Algy, and even Ben, always knew when I was unhappy, and left their happy hunting along the banks and huddled close to me, so that we all sat together, a miserable little bunch, with a girl in the centre. I think that never in my whole life have I suffered more deeply than I did then, as a child, with my heart full of terror for my dearly-loved dog. I put my face against his strong golden neck and wept bitterly.

That night I didn't sleep at all, and I kept my hand hanging over the edge of my bed, touching Ajax. I was thankful when the night was over and Ajax was still safe. But the calves were safe too, so that proved really nothing.

A watch had been kept on the yards, and this was to go on until the moon waned in three or four nights. The watchers sat in the little cowshed where big cracks in the roughly-timbered walls gave them a view of the yard, while they were invisible in the darkness within. A loaded rifle leant against the wall.

The day dragged on and I forced myself to lie awake and keep my vigil on Ajax the next night, The third night, try as I would to rouse myself, in the end I fell asleep – and woke to the terror of knowing that Ajax was not there!

I jumped out of bed and scrambled into my sandals and warm dressing-gown, and stole out of the house. Of course Algy and Ben tried to follow me, but I sent them back so firmly that they gazed at me in amazement as I shut the gate. Then I ran towards the yard as quickly as I could. The distance between the house and the milking shed was bathed in the ghostly light of the moon, silver white and coldly horrible to me that night, and I've never liked moonlight very much since then. Once, far in the distance, I was sure I could see a big form loping towards the yards.

For a little while I could hear the dogs snuffling and whining at the gate behind me, and my feet crunched on the crisp, frosty grass as the blades poked through the open straps of my sandals, and my feet got wetter and colder as I ran on. Again, I thought I saw Ajax circling the yards in the far distance.

I reached the fence and began creeping round the wooden railings towards the shed, which was between me and the huddled calves. The cold, platinum light of the moon gave me the sense of being quite alone in a vast, desolate world. Hugging the wooden walls of the shed, I crept softly to the door, and *sssshd* at Lewis and my father before they could exclaim at my appearance.

Then followed what seemed like hours of waiting, but it probably was not more than half an hour. Outside the calves were restless, but kept tightly packed together. We three crouched in the little shed, and presently we heard the thud of running feet. There was the jarring sound of a heavy body on soft wood, and on top of the railings we saw a huge, honey-coloured shape, its fiery gold bleached by the moonlight – Ajax!

My heart thudded and I felt sick. I wanted to call him but I did not dare. I knew that what had to be done *must* be done. Lewis picked up the rifle silently, and the wicked muzzle pointed through a crack. The calves milled and churned in their corner. I closed my eyes and I prayed very hard. Then I felt my father's hand on my shoulder and I opened my eyes.

The moonlight shone down on Ajax, an Ajax that I did not know. Gone was his proud and splendid bearing. His tongue lolled from his mouth as he moved towards the frightened calves with short mincing steps that had an indescribable evil about them.

Then I wondered if I was going mad, for at almost the same spot on the rails appeared another huge dog. Gaunt and golden he hung there for a moment, streaked by the silver of the moonlight, and then dropped to the ground. The creeping dog turned, and they stood for a moment facing each other, and even the ground seemed to vibrate to the low, shuddering rumble of their growls, sounds that were infinitely more dangerous than the snarls and yelps of lesser dogs.

Then the first dog sprang like an overstretched spring, so swiftly that to my eyes he seemed just a blur of light. The other dog's shoulder opened in a great gash, and his blood was black in the moonlight. He whirled like light, and this time it was the first dog's shoulder that was gashed. Sometimes we could hear the clash of their teeth as a swift wolf-slash missed its mark, at other times there was no sound, but another of those terrible gashes opened and blood flowed down. I turned to Lewis and said despairingly:

'Lewis – help Ajax!'

'Dear little girl, I can't, I don't know which dog *is* Ajax.'

'If I call him?'

'No! No, you mustn't do that – if you distract his attention he may be killed –'

Both dogs were covered in wounds, then, suddenly, one huge body hurtled through the air. In a moment the other's teeth met in his opponent's throat, the great legs twitched, and then the dog lay still. The victorious fighter lifted his bleeding muzzle from his victim's throat and gave a deep, long wolf-call of victory.

I couldn't stand it any longer, and I called:

'Ajax!'

The dog's long, haunting cry broke, and he turned his head in a puzzled sort of way, almost as if he'd been asleep. I called again, and the bloodstained figure turned towards my voice, the rifle was lowered, and my dog Ajax lifted his caked muzzle to me to be caressed.

I insisted on going with the others to look at Ajax's dead enemy. My father murmured:

'It is impossible to tell them apart!'

Lewis examined the fallen yellow carcass closely, then he mentioned the dead pup we had found in the log before we got to Ajax, and said:

'This must be the third pup – I expect it ran into the log last, and wriggled out again while Ajax was blocked in by the dead body of his brother.'

'Then Ajax has killed his brother,' I said sadly, for I could not help thinking what a wonderful dog someone might have had, if this one had been given the same chance as Ajax.

'They obviously belong to the same family,' Lewis answered, 'but this one ran wild while Ajax was tamed – sort of,' he added, smiling down into Ajax's very untamed eyes.

'Circumstantial evidence very nearly did for you, old boy!' my father said, putting his hand gently on Ajax's torn head. Then I told them about the blood under Ajax's jaw that I'd found after that first night, for now it was obvious that he'd been examining his brother's victims.

Ajax had lost a lot of blood and his wounds were stiffening, but he walked home beside me with his old, proud step, and allowed me to attend to the worst of his wounds without a whimper. Then, with my dog beside me, I climbed into bed, and slept soundly for the first time for three nights.

8. Mitta Comes to Stay

I was very shy when my mother's friends brought their children to stay. The fact was that I simply didn't know how to play with other children, and I used rather to dread their arrival. It seemed to me they often lacked proper respect for Algy, Ben and Ajax; my pony, Buck, always tried to throw strange children off, and, rather unfairly, I was sometimes blamed for this, probably because I never liked them to ride him anyway. My contention was that strange children spoilt his paces, but that was a great stretch of imagination, for Buck had no paces. His one idea, when ridden, was to do as many unpleasant things as possible, and these consisted of shying, jogging and bolting, so that the rider would get fed up, and then he would be allowed to come home and get back to the serious business of eating and sleeping.

I was always glad when my visitors left, and I could go back to my solitary ways again. There was one exception to this, but she was very unlike an ordinary visitor for I found her myself; her name was Mitta, and she was coal-black.

You can't go very fast sailing up a river in a flat-bottomed, home-made boat with a complicated arrangement of broom-stick, rope, and your father's shirt to act as sail, but you can have a lot of fun. A shirt is a very good small sail because the arms tie nicely on to the mast. The dogs and I had great fun, and when we were tired of sailing I would take the big, clumsy oars and drive the boat through the curtain of willows that screened both sides of the river banks, and then we would sleep and laze in the speckled shade.

One day I was doing just this and the dogs were sound asleep around me on the floor of the boat, when, without the slightest sound, I opened my eyes because I felt the boat tilt a little towards one side. The dogs felt it too, and Ajax woke growling, and Benny went into a frenzy of barks, but not before I'd seen a pair of small black hands, a dripping black head and big black eyes appear for an instant above the side. I jumped up and so did the dogs, and the boat rocked wildly; there was no sign of the owner of the hands, hair and eyes. I quietened the dogs and looked around. There was nothing to be seen. But what I could not see Ajax could; he sprang into the water and swam towards the trunk of one of the willows, and from behind it came screams of 'Missie! Missie!' and a wail of fear. I called out: 'It's all right – Ajax won't hurt you!' and picked up an oar and pushed the boat towards the tree. The screams went on and I could see branches waving wildly as a scrambling went on among the greenery. Then I made out the wet, shiny blackness of a little girl a good deal smaller than myself.

Ajax was paddling about, treading water and looking up at her in an interested way, until she stopped screaming and began scolding him, throwing down twigs and small branches. I made Ajax climb back into the boat, and with the three dogs sitting there and staring in great surprise I tried to reassure her and invited her into the boat.

I don't think I would have been able to persuade her except for some fruit I had brought with me, and I held this up to her. She began to climb down slowly, talking and scolding all the time in her odd, pidgin English, and I pushed the boat into the bank and waited for her with my hand on Ajax's and Algy's necks. She had been so occupied with Ajax that I think she had not even noticed Algy, and when he did catch her rolling black eyes, she made as if to rush back up the tree again. Finally I held out an apricot to her, and she came near enough to grab it, and then wolfed it down, gurgling:

'Tank you please.'

It took a long time to persuade her that the dogs would not hurt her, and I put them out on the bank and invited her into the boat. When it was time to go home she still sat nervously in the stern, stark naked, and very pleased with herself for being so brave about the dogs.

I got out of the boat and walked up the bank, calling the dogs back from their rabbiting, and when I got back, the sail, my father's old shirt that was, was already draping Mitta. She was obviously taking a great pride in her costume, crooning to herself and patting her thin little arms inside the sleeves that hung down past her knees. The shirt would have held half a dozen Mittas, and the tail dragged on the ground, but I could see that it would not be any use trying to retrieve it and replace the sail, and that I had better make up my mind to row all the way home. The river was rising from the heavy rains above, and even in the short time I had been anchored it had come up more than a foot; as the way home was downstream, the confiscated sail did not matter very much.

But what did matter was returning Mitta to her family, wherever they might be. I gathered vaguely that they were somewhere up-river and would not worry about her, and that she had no intention of losing her new playmate before she had inspected every inch of my 'humpy', which is what she called my home.

So I took Mitta home with me, and walked in closely followed by this strange little figure, looking like a thin

'It's all right – Ajax won't hurt you!'

Roman in a fat Roman's toga, her black face shining with interest and excitement as she examined what was to her a wonderful 'humpy' of many rooms and strange furnishings.

My mother was very surprised, to say the least of it, but it had begun to pour with rain, so it was certain that Mitta could not be sent home until it cleared a bit. Then we discovered that Mitta had not the least idea where her home was. She only knew that it was on the other side of the river. Her father was a cattle drover, and about a year before this he had taken his family from away up in the Northern Territory, and had brought a mob of cattle many hundreds of miles southward. By the time the mob was delivered, Dad was apparently so fascinated by civilization that he decided to go on southward, instead of returning home.

So Mitta, Mum and Dad and several younger piccaninnies began a sort of hitch-hiking tour towards the New South Wales – Queensland border. Sometimes teamsters would give the family a lift in an empty wagon, and once or twice they had the wonderful thrill of being allowed to travel in an empty cattle truck. This journey, supplemented by walking probably hundreds of miles, young children and all, had ended when they settled a few miles above Gunyan, and Mitta, bent on exploring, had arrived near the homestead itself when she had seen me sailing up the river with the dogs, and had decided to investigate the whole thing.

Mitta's amazement at my playroom and toys was wonderful to see, and when I told her she could have Flo for her very own she was busting with delight. Flo was actually my favourite toy; she was a smart lady in a pink leg-o'-mutton-sleeved silk blouse, and a straw hat tied beneath her chin with a veil, a long grey skirt and buttoned boots, and she rode a clockwork tricycle. Mitta was completely dumbfounded when Flo came to life after being wound up, and it was fun to see this miniature cycling English lady riding briskly round and round, and the tiny black girl gazing at her in ecstasy, her eyes so wide that the bluish whites surrounded the pupils. When Flo stopped because she ran down, Mitta sat gloomily shaking her head and saying:

'Flo dead-fellow now!'

My mother came in bringing some clothes of mine that I'd grown out of, but Mitta refused to give up the shirt. After much persuasion she allowed us to put on a pink linen dress, but only when she was promised that she could have the shirt too, to take home with her.

The rain still beat down, and the river was rising very rapidly and was already uncrossable. My father said we must keep Mitta until the flood subsided and she could find her way home, or until we could send someone to find her father and to tell him to come and get her. So that is how Mitta and I settled down to a week of very happy companionship, and to a friendship that lasted until Mitta's family 'went bush' again.

She was a dear little girl, and her ways and games were much more like my own than were those of white children. When Mitta got over her fear of the dogs she was rather inclined to show off about it, even smacking them, to my great annoyance, when she decided that they had been naughty. She loved to swagger up to Ajax and throw her arms round his neck, or climb on to his back. He never did more than growl at her, but he used to give me the most agonized looks! Algy rather enjoyed being scolded and crawled over. Benny was much too agile for her, and he kept his distance, but she did not mind, because to her Benny was just an ordinary mutt, while Ajax and Algy were something special.

Then one day she went a bit too far. I had gone inside for something when I heard shrieks from the garden:

'Mitta bin kill Algy! Mitta bin kill Algy!'

This was too much. I rushed out and found Mitta standing on the lawn, a long switch in her hand, screaming about killing Algy, who was nowhere in sight. In my anxiety I shook her hard, she calmed down, and I discovered she had been swishing her switch around and had hit Algy with it, and he had yelped and run away. Then I called Algy and he came sheepishly from behind a tree. I made Mitta make much of him, and said:

'You mustn't ever do that again – but you haven't *killed* him!' But Mitta kept on nodding her head and repeating, 'Mitta killed Algy,' until finally I realized that to her 'kill' meant 'hurt,' but to really *kill* as we know it was to 'make deadfellow'.

Mitta wasn't exactly hygienic in her habits, in spite of her nightly bath in front of the kitchen fire. She rather liked this attention, but if my mother tried to wash her face or hair with soap she would scream:

'No! No! Missus! Soap bitum eyes!' and then she would fight like a little wildcat against it. Then she would get proudly into one of my nightgowns and have her supper with me. But when it was bed-time nothing would make her get into the camp bed on the verandah which my mother had fixed for her, nor would she keep the precious nightgown on. She would turn down the bed, the way she had been shown, and then take off the nightgown, roll it up and put it under the pillow, and lie down, completely naked, on the floor, curled round like a scraggy little puppy, and sleep soundly.

I loved the bush and I thought I knew many of its ways, but Mitta taught me more. On one head-washing occasion my mother found a nest of her own hairpins hidden in Mitta's hair, and Mitta would not say why she wanted them, so my mother simply gave them to her to put back in her hair. The next day Mitta was very mysterious, and we went down to the river bank and she found a bush-oak and began tearing away the bark with her little hands. Presently she found what she wanted, and taking a hairpin from the nest in her hair she bored and dug into the soft wood under the bark. Then she triumphantly extracted a fat white grub. With a shriek of delight she went vigorously to work, pressing another hairpin into my hands, but I really did not like piercing the grubs, so I struck, and just watched her.

When she had four or five she searched for a bit of dry hardwood and a pointed stick, then she made a fire as only an Abo can. It only seemed seconds when the twirling point of wood on a dry chip struck a spark. She fed it carefully, and soon had a tiny fire. Then she skewered the unfortunate grubs and toasted them, offering me my share, but was very delighted when I refused! Mitta ate the horrid things with every sign of relish, but that was a bush lesson I never wanted to repeat!

The gramophone was a never-ending source of mystery and delight to Mitta. Whenever we played it to her she made a thorough search, behind and in it, for the voice. It was one of those old ones with a very big aluminium horn that was as tall as Mitta herself, and very light. One night, when the rain clouds had cleared away and a full moon shone down, I heard unearthly sounds coming from the garden. I hurried out of bed and the dogs and I ran into my parents, and we all went to the windows in the front of the house. I was half asleep and I hadn't noticed that Mitta wasn't with us but when we all crowded round the windows and looked into the moonlight we saw why. Like a little black Bacchante, Mitta was prancing about the lawn. Her thin arms held up the gramophone horn that was as tall as herself, and she chanted and shouted her weird tribal music through it, stamping and staggering, and enjoying herself no end.

'Let her play,' my mother said, 'she'll soon tire herself out, and she seems to be enjoying it very much!'

So we all went back to bed, and after a while there was silence, and soon Mitta threw herself down in her usual place, still hugging the gramophone horn, and slept until morning.

I learned some of the myths of the Northern blacks from Mitta, myths that had no meaning any more for our more civilized tribes in the south. Once, when a rainbow appeared in the watery sky, she rushed to a spot which she said was the end of it, and began digging furiously. Not knowing what it was all about, I began to dig too, and Mitta refused to stop until we were both exhausted. Then, as we squatted back on our heels, panting, she seemed very disappointed. When I inquired what she was looking for in the big, muddy hole we had dug, she said:

'Piccaninny-fellow rainbow.'

Naturally I was very disappointed that we hadn't found a baby rainbow, and often wondered to myself what it would have been like. When I was older I read that some Northern tribes think that hailstones are rainbows' eggs. When these melt into the ground they believe that they hatch out into baby rainbows. These are the small worms with brightly-coloured stripes that live in the wet earth. I felt that our southern rainbows and earth did not have half the interesting features of the northern ones.

My mother had one of those dressmaking stands that look like wire cages as far as the hips, and this interested Mitta very much. It was obvious that she was convinced that it was really alive, just as, to her, Flo was alive when I wound her up – a thing Mitta would never do for herself. It looked rather like half a human because I had stuck the head of a large doll on top of the wire neck, and dressed the rest in an old blouse that came down to the table on which this curious apparition sat. Mitta would push the blouse gingerly aside with a small black finger, and peer into its empty vitals, looking very worried all the time. This skeleton lady stood on the sewing table, and one day when my mother wanted to use it and lifted it from the table the most extraordinary collection of scraps of food fell all over the place. Mitta, sure that the poor hollow thing must be hungry, had been feeding it whenever possible, poking the food through the wires!

Mitta really won my whole heart when she saved Ben from a black snake. These deadly poisonous snakes were a great anxiety to me with the dogs. I tried to teach them to shun every snake, but I suppose they were so used to seeing me play with Kaa, my harmless old carpet snake, that they never quite understood that other snakes were not so harmless. One day Mitta and I were walking along the thick, leafy earth at the river's edge, when just ahead of us a small black snake began to come out of the water. These snakes are great swimmers and dangerous enough in the water, but much faster and more deadly out of it. In droughty times, when the river gets choked with water weeds, you often find black snakes drowning in thick patches of weed they cannot swim out of, or you turn them up on the blade of an oar. They have slate-black backs, and the male snakes are a brilliant red underneath, while the females have bellies of lighter slate blue than their backs.

I called the dogs to me, but Master Ben, bent on being naughty, took no notice, and rushed ahead of us straight at the snake. I had one hand each on Ajax and Algy and called despairingly to Ben to come to heel, but Mitta did not wait for Ben; like a little black eel she flung herself at the snake's tail just as it was coming out of the water, snatched it away from Ben's nose, and cracked it as a man would crack a stockwhip, breaking its neck, which is the way Abos always kill snakes. Then Mitta knotted it around her in what she no doubt thought was a graceful neckpiece, and we went on our way. When I tried to thank her she did not seem to know what I was talking about, but just remarked cheerfully:

'Him cheeky-fellow snake, Missie,' and pranced on. Kaa, according to Mitta, was not a 'cheeky-fellow' snake, so I suppose that term was reserved for the poisonous varieties.

We had all grown very fond of Mitta, and I was very sad when the river subsided and my father sent one of the men up river on the Queensland side, with orders to find Mitta's family. He found them living in a bark 'humpy', the walls eked out with kerosene tins beaten flat, and they all came down to the station to collect the wayward daughter. Apparently they had not been in the least worried about her; she was a child of the bush, and it never occurred to them to think that anything might have happened to her.

We gave them a feast with lots of meat and sticky sweets, all the piccaninnies got toys, and, thinking of Benny, I let Mitta take just what she wanted from my own toys. She was not at all greedy, and, except for Flo, those she liked best were not my own favourites.

Finally, laden with meat and tinned foods, old clothes and toys, the little tribe went back to their humpy, but until they 'went bush' some months afterwards Mitta was with me more than she was at home, even though every visit meant a fresh bath with soap to 'bitum eyes'.

9. Ajax Catches a Horse Thief

Soon after I met Mitta my mother managed to get a governess for me. 'Brownie' was a darling, an Englishwoman who really loved my dogs almost as much as I did. My lessons were not very serious, only nine to twelve, and with frequent holidays, so I soon settled down and began to enjoy them.

Matilda, my kangaroo, had been christened from the song 'Waltzing Matilda', for the rolled swag on a sundowner's back was called a 'Matilda'. These men, whom we called 'swaggies', used to tramp through the Australian bush, taking jobs only when they needed money, and every station gave them a ration of foods, and these rations were very substantial ones with tea, sugar, flour, and pounds of meat. This custom really began in the early pioneering days in Australia when hundreds of empty miles stretched between properties, with little traffic and less water, and these swagmen often died of hunger and thirst.

Many swaggies called at Gunyan, collected their rations, talked a while, and then wandered off to the next station. They were not bad lots, just restless men who loved to wander, but of course there was an occasional bad one who took his rations and then robbed the hen-house or garden. I only remember one real criminal, but he did not get away with it for long – thanks to Ajax, and to Mitta's father Billy, who was an excellent black tracker.

One of my father's greatest interests was picnic racing, for which the horses came from the best blood-stock and were always ridden by amateurs. Every year we had two days' racing, a day of polo, tennis and dancing, and there was always a houseful of guests – I can remember as many as forty people in my home at these times. Of course there was great rivalry among the horse owners for the splendid prizes. My mother had a great deal of jewellery that my father's horses had won for her.

The horses were not raced until they were two-year-olds, and one year my father had a very successful bay mare called 'Frasca'. We were very proud of her, and when all the excitement happened Frasca was being groomed for her second year of racing, with the big meeting in about three weeks' time.

I came home one evening, after the dogs and I had spent our afternoon by the river, and I saw my great friend Lewis standing talking to a stranger. He was a dilapidated creature, a real swaggie, and so I walked over because I liked them very much, and loved their stories. I said 'Good evening', and the man grunted something and gave me a surly look. I did not like his face nor his grumpy voice, so I had turned to walk away when Ajax walked stiff-legged towards the man growling in his throat. I realized that Ajax was frightening when you did not know him, so I stopped and said to the man:

'Ajax won't hurt you – he always grumbles like that. Come on, Ajax!'

The man turned towards Ajax, and with an ugly look on his face he said:

'Too right he won't hurt me!'

Then before I could answer he kicked out and caught Ajax in the ribs, a heavy, sickening kick. I was so astounded that I stood for a second gaping, before I even felt furious. I think that Ajax was completely surprised too, in all his life no one had ever done such a thing before; so he hesitated an instant, and then, with his lips drawn back in his terrible fighter's grin, and his teeth gleaming white in the dusk, he sprang straight at the man, who went over backwards under the weight of the dog. For an instant I saw Ajax astride the man, his wolf's jaws holding the man's throat, and I saw, too, the terrified expression in the man's eyes. Then Lewis and I moved together, and with my arms round Ajax's neck we dragged him away.

The man got to his feet swearing at the dog. Ajax's teeth had bruised his throat, but had not broken the skin. Lewis told him to shut up, he had brought it on himself, he was lucky that Ajax had not torn his throat out. I was holding Ajax and trembling so much with rage that I could not control myself:

'Get out! Get your rations and get away from here – how *dare* you touch my Ajax – get out – or – or I'll sic him on to you!'

The man looked as if he would have liked to kill us all, but he was frightened, supposing that I could not hold Ajax – or that I did not want to. Then I heard Lewis say:

'Come on, I'll get your rations, then get on your way – and don't you ever come back again.'

They went into the store-house. I was terribly upset and examined Ajax carefully. It had been a hard kick, but Ajax was tough and no bones were broken. I could only hold the great head in my hands to tell him how sorry I was. My mother often talked to me about Ajax, he was so big and strong and had all the instincts of his wild breed, and she told me that never in his life must he know anything but love and kindness. Up to then he never had, and I could not bear to think that he had been hurt so treacherously.

In the morning the man was gone – and so was my father's beautiful mare, Frasca.

As in all pioneer countries, the stealing of any kind of stock is a serious crime; then, too, we loved Frasca, and she was a valuable thoroughbred, and by far the finest of my father's horses. So Lewis set off up-river to find Mitta's father. All blacks are wonderful trackers by our standards, far better than any white man; they can follow a trail where ordinary sharp eyes cannot see the faintest mark. Soon Lewis came back with Billy, and we all went along to Frasca's empty stable. The man could easily be fifty miles away by night time. As I loved watching Billy track, my father said I could ride part of the way with them.

At the stables Ajax got very restless and cast about, growling in his throat. I thought he might mix up the tracks for Billy, but he said to leave him alone. My brother and I used to love to hide from Ajax, but he always found us very quickly, and then he would give me such a disapproving look, as much as to say:

'Do stop trying these silly tricks on me.'

So Billy thought Ajax might be useful to him. Billy tracked on foot, and like all Abos he could cover fifty or sixty miles at a tireless lope. He was a thin, wiry man, his face the mulberry-black of the true Abo, with a flat nose and lank hair; he wore a torn old pair of trousers, and his calloused, splay-toed feet were bare.

Algy and Ben were most aggrieved when I made them stay at home because I did not know how far I would be going. We saddled our horses and followed Billy. For once Ajax seemed to forget me; he sniffed and cast along the trail with a single-mindedness that made me sure he knew that it belonged to the man who had kicked him the evening before. I felt afraid of what he might do if he found the man first, and I told my father this. He said, 'Let the dog alone – we'll keep up with him.'

We cantered along and found Billy standing looking

very puzzled at the river's edge. Water is one thing that stumps even a black tracker – for a while. The man might have crossed, or he might have ridden along the edge in either direction.

Then we heard Ajax's deep voice somewhere up river, so with Billy trotting along the edge we rode our horses up the bank and cantered along to find Ajax baying at us from a shallow, pebbled crossing. Even Billy could see nothing, but Ajax seemed so sure that we followed him across. And then began a game of hide-and-seek that went on for hours. Eventually we found that the man had doubled back towards the homestead again, evidently thinking that this would stump us – he had probably reckoned without either Billy or Ajax. And then, about five miles from home, the trail led us towards a jumble of rocks called Mooroobie's Cave. 'Mooroobie' is an Abo word for a death-adder, that sleepy deadly adder that lives in rocky places. We often picnicked there, and there were no more adders than there were in any rocky spot.

The Mooroobie rocks differed from other outcrops, for on top of a rocky hillside there were huge oblong stones, not unlike the pillars at Stonehenge, and these were jumbled about, forming a shallow cave with a sort of rocky lintel across the front, and a low wall of rocks hiding the cave.

I was tired, my father tried to send me home, but I would not leave Ajax. No one expected to catch up with the man that day, and so my father let me stay. Now he worried about me because, as we stopped in a clump of trees, we saw a thin spiral of smoke going up from the top of the hillock, and we knew that it must be the thief. I got off my horse as my father, Billy, Lewis and one of the stockmen talked together. There was no sign of the mare, but we knew that the thief could have hidden her somewhere among the rocks.

Ajax sprang straight on the man's back.

The men all carried rifles, and with his on his arm my father walked out from the trees and went towards the rocks calling:

'Hi! You! Come on, come out of there, I want to talk to you!'

There was no answer. My father called again, and when there was still no answer he aimed at the top of the rocks and the bullet chipped a bit off, and went whining into the distance. That did it. From behind the rocks a man stood up, and the sun glinted along the barrel of his rifle. He shouted back that if they wanted him they would have to come and get him. My father kept on walking towards the rocks and a bullet tore up the earth at his feet. He stood still, leaning on his gun, and talking to the man.

It was then, peering through the trees and feeling very frightened for my father, that I noticed that Ajax was not beside me. I was torn between anxiety for my father and worry over Ajax when Lewis touched my arm and pointed to the side of the rocks where the man stood shouting back at my father.

There I saw my dog, but he was not the dog I knew; this was an untamed hunter pursuing his enemy. Like a shadow he crept forward, absolutely soundless in spite of the loose stones. Then I saw the great body leap with a feathery lightness on to the rock we called the lintel. It was above the man's head, and about four feet behind him. For an instant Ajax crouched there, and I knew that my father must have been watching him, and that he had gone on talking purposely. Then, like an arc of golden light, Ajax sprang straight on to the man's back. He yelled with fear, the rifle clattered down the outer rocks, and man and dog disappeared behind the big front rock. There was a deathly, frightening silence.

Lewis tried to hold me, but I tore myself away and

ran as fast as I could towards the rocks, while my father and the men raced behind me. I was filled with fear for Ajax – if he had killed the man then he would have destroyed himself too. In an agony of terror I scrambled over the rocks, and because I was small and light and agile as a monkey, and because I knew every rock on the hillock, I was the first to reach the top.

There, stretched in front of the rock, was the same tableau I had seen the night before – the man on his back, surly-faced and frightened-eyed, and over him standing my dog, an ominous rumble in his great chest, his eyes full of wild light, and his muzzle drawn back in his grinning, wolf's snarl.

It was all right – the man was alive! I stood there a moment, panting myself, afraid to call Ajax before the men arrived. As soon as they stepped on to the rock with their rifles ready, I put my hand on my dog's head. Still growling, he stepped backwards off the man's body, and we could see that the thief was quite unhurt except for a few bruises.

After the man was tied up I searched for Frasca, and found her tethered between two rocks halfway up the hill. I led her down and rode on ahead, keeping Ajax with me, and left the men to cope with the brutal horse-thief, who was made to cover the five miles of rough ground on foot, before being handed over to the police for trial.

10. Benny in the Limelight

Brownie, my governess, made a special pet of Benny, probably because he was so small; but after Ajax caught the horse-thief he got a lot of attention he did not particularly want. Benny was very jealous, and I am sure he was delighted when his own adventures turned people's attention back to him again. Benny always wanted to do everything the 'big boys' did, and he loved to go mustering with me.

In the ordinary work on a cattle station mustering means riding out perhaps twenty miles to collect the cattle together, perhaps for a cattle buyer. The cattle are mustered into what are called 'camps', flat pieces of ground inside a semi-circle of fencing. Perhaps five hundred head are driven in here, stockmen and dogs keep them from getting out at the open side, and the buyer rides in among them and points out which beasts he wants. Then a stockman rides into the herd, and 'cuts out' the chosen beasts. These are driven a little way into the open, to form a smaller herd of their own, until they are all gathered together and driven off to their destination.

'Cutting out' is great fun; the stockhorses push the chosen beasts with their shoulders, twisting and turning with them until finally they separate them from the rest of the herd. My fat bay pony Buck was quite good among the stock, until it grew hot and the milling cattle raised the dust. Then he would get very bored, and if I was unreasonable about resting when he felt like it he would turn his head and nip me. This was easy to do, because until I was older I never rode in a saddle, and when Buck was in a nipping mood I had to scramble about his broad back to get out of reach of his nips – which really were a bit much!

Dear old Algy was too big to follow and too big to carry for long rides, though Ajax was tireless, and Master Ben made a to-do if he was left at home, and always ended by galloping after me on his short legs, sniffing the hoof-tracks like a bloodhound that by some enchantment had shrunk into a small, silky bundle. So the naughty little dog usually got his own way, and when he was tired he would perch in front of me, on the saddle, yelping whenever he sighted a rabbit or a kangaroo rat hopping through the grass.

When I first graduated from Buck to my beautiful chestnut mare Belle she made a great fuss when Ben was handed up to me; but she soon got used to him, and Master Ben fancied himself terrifically as a horseman, and used to sit with his front paws on the mare's neck and his little rump on the flat pommel that stock saddles have, his hind legs dangling on either side. It seems mean to add that I steadied him with my right hand all the time and it exasperated him very much!

Ajax, who used to make sorties through the long grass whenever he suspected anything would interest him, used to cover probably thirty miles or more, and when we got home he would fling himself down and go off to sleep. But Ben, who had spent more than half the time riding and was not a bit tired, used to show off, running about and playing with Algy, and casting withering looks at the sleeping Ajax.

One day we rode home in the cool of the evening, almost too tired to enjoy the evening laughter of the kookaburras. These are the most fascinating birds, with big, fluffy heads, small bodies and wedge-shaped tails.

They usually have a laughing match morning and evening, beginning with chuckling sounds and rising to shouts of laughter. This evening they were laughing all around us, and Ben, who was most exasperatingly lively, spied a rabbit and wriggled and struggled so that I thought, 'Very well, my boy, if you have all that energy just you go and chase your rabbit!' So I slid him to the ground over my foot and off he went, yap-yap after the rabbit.

I was nearly asleep with tiredness when I looked around to see if Ben wanted to be picked up again, and he was not there. I called out to the stockmen riding ahead of me, and they told me not to worry, we were only walking our tired horses and Ben would be sure to catch us up. After another mile, and no sign of Ben, I felt too worried to go on, and called to the men not to wait as I was going back to call Ben. We were only a mile or so from home, so I turned the tired, reluctant mare and called Ajax. We went back calling 'Benny!' every few yards. He never came. It was getting very dark, for there is no twilight in Australia, and the dark comes like a swiftly-dropped curtain. There was no moon, and the clear sky full of brilliant stars gave little light.

Finally there was nothing for it but to ride home. I was terribly worried, but I knew I must have light and help to search further if Ben, as I thought, was stuck in a hollow log.

I rode wearily home; my father said I must go to bed and at daylight we would all go to search for Ben. Dear old Algy kept running around and sniffing in the corners, obviously missing Benny very much, while the heartless Ajax went sound asleep. I thought that I would not sleep a wink, imagining my little fellow frightened and hungry, perhaps injured, but I was so tired that I did fall asleep very quickly.

At dawn I awoke, called my father and Lewis, and we caught and saddled the horses. As it was not far we decided to take Algy, feeling that the dogs had a much better chance of finding Ben than we had. We had an early breakfast and set off.

Usually I loved early-morning bush rides, but that morning I was too worried to enjoy the pale spears of sunlight like a flight of honey-golden arrows going away in the distance, as the sun swept up from below the horizon. Soon it was brazenly hot and the vivid blue of the skies pressed down on our heads. The mare jingled her bit and curtsied at her shadow, but I was too worried to enjoy it. We went slowly on account of Algy, but it was not long before we turned off the dusty road and the horses stepped delicately among fallen boughs and rabbit holes. We spread out and called to Ben every little while, and the dogs ran and sniffed and toured in wide circles, but they had no luck. We went on searching until it was nearly noon and the heat was scorching, dry, Australian heat that seems to burn as you breathe it in, and then we turned sadly homewards. My father and Lewis tried to comfort me, saying that even now Ben might just turn up at the homestead. But I could not be comforted.

Even Ajax seemed worried, and he kept very close to me as he always did when he thought that I was unhappy, and did not growl when unhappy Algy tried to climb into my lap. Algy hung over my small lap every way, but he seemed to be soothed by the idea that he was a puppy again, so I put my arms round him to hold up the overlapping bits, and it seemed to comfort him as much as it comforted me.

That horrible day crawled by, and when it was a little cooler we went back to the place we had last seen Benny. This time we took the car, and left it on the road while we walked slowly among stumps, and trees, and holes, but it was no use.

Next morning I got up before daylight, saddled my mare, and the dogs and I went back towards where we had last seen Ben, then turned and went up beside a fence for about a mile, for I decided to double back and comb the country towards the road instead of away from it. I had a water-bottle on my saddle, and gave the dogs a little, saving the rest for Ben – if we found him. I led Belle and walked in wide circles, calling, and examining every hole and rotted log on the way.

After a couple of hours of this I was very weary, my feet hurt and all my discouragement and misery rushed over me. I threw myself down in a piece of the sparse shade, turned on my face and cried miserably. Presently I felt Algy snuffling at me, licking my ear, snorting and nudging at me, and I thought he was just trying to comfort me. He kept it up, and presently I realized that all this business meant something. He trotted off a few steps, barking; I sat up, he was looking back at me and making the snorting noises he always did when he wanted me to follow him, so I got up and obliged. Then he seemed to lose his way, and rushed hither and thither, panting and blowing, and finally stood head down, yelping excitedly. I ran over to him, and he had his blunt nose stuck down the hole of a rabbit burrow. He sniffed and began to dig.

I bent down and called: 'Ben! Ben!' There was no answer and I called again. I thought I heard an answering whine! It was only a tiny sound, but it *was* a sound – I was sure of it! I pushed Algy away and dug my hands into the earth. It was packed and hard, I tore my hands and broke my nails, but I could not dig it away. So I stood up and looked about for something with which to mark the spot. When I found a stick I tied my handkerchief to the top and dug it in the earth. Ajax was sniffing about the hole, but I would not let him dig because if the burrow were very honeycombed he might make the earth crash down on to Ben – if it was Ben!

Algy was a problem. If I left him he would be sure to dig, and if I took him with us he would slow us up so much. In the end I hurt his feelings by taking off a stirrup-leather and tying him to a tree. I felt a brute, for he had never been tied up before, and he gazed sadly at me wondering what he had done to deserve this, while I jumped on the mare and tore for home in my stirrupless saddle. For once I let the mare gallop full out, but she never outdistanced Ajax, who loped easily beside me the whole way.

When I arrived home a stable-boy took the mare, Lewis brought shovels, and I rushed to the kitchen and filled one bottle with milk and another with water, and we were ready. Ajax and I bundled into the car, Lewis drove, and we reached the spot in no time. Algy rushed about delightedly when I freed him and as usual bore me no malice. I ran to where my handkerchief waved above the grass, and I bent down and called to Ben, but there was no answer, and I was very afraid.

Lewis began digging carefully, following the wind-burrow, but the ground was very hard and many passages led off from the main one. After about half an hour's hard digging we came to what seemed to be a fall of earth. We scraped this out with our hands, and there, behind the loose earth in a little pocket of space, was my Ben – not the lively bully we knew, but a weary, bedraggled little dog that for once wanted to be petted and made much of.

He was very weak, there had not been much air in the passageway, and he was very dirty. Algy was beside himself with delight and nuzzled and licked

Benny joyously, and even Ajax unbent enough to come over and take a look at Ben to make sure he was all right. I carried the little dog to the car and gave him some milk and water. The little fellow was terribly thirsty. Then I dipped my handkerchief in the water and wiped some of the dust and caked dirt from around his eyes and jaws. He actually settled down on my knee in the car, and we stopped once to give him another drink.

I was so happy at having the little chap that I could not speak. Poor Benny, what he must have suffered from heat and thirst imprisoned in that sun-baked earth no one knows. Probably this should have been a lesson to him against being so cocksure, but it was not. By the time we reached home, not half an hour after he'd been rescued, he was trying to struggle upright on my knee, and to give a feeble ghost of his usual shrill yap when he sighted everyone lined up to welcome him! He really was very weak, and when I put him in his basket beside my bed he was quite happy to call it a day, and to go straight off to sleep. Dusty and dirty as he was, I felt that a bath should wait until he was his arrogant self, and he could snap at the soap bubbles, scold me, and squirm away, wet and slippery as an eel, to roll himself dry on the lawn.

11. Benny to the Rescue

Of course Benny was outrageously spoilt after so nearly being lost for good, and one way and another he managed to keep himself in the limelight most of the summer – mainly because my brother and I taught Benny a trick because he was such a little show-off, and enjoyed doing it so much. We would tie a message to his neck and tell him to carry it to one or other of us, or to Lewis or my father, and very soon he learned to dash from one to the other feeling very important. In the end he would gallop half a mile on his fat little legs and deliver the message faithfully.

It was a dry summer, and the muddy river-water lay as still as a lake beneath the low bank, and the water was almost too discoloured to reflect the elegant trunks of the silver gums that grew behind the willow trees lining the banks. Their branches ended in a tangled growth on the surface of the water, and water-fowl would nest in them; I loved to watch the small black hens scurrying along half-submerged logs on tiny bright red feet, or swimming near the bank, followed by the fluffy blobs of their water-wise brood. I would squat on a log and watch the chicks and the defiant water-spiders skating round my finger-tips, or peer into the bottle-green water, looking for the ghostly, transparent forms of fresh-water shrimps that you can see clinging to submerged logs, while above them, the water closed sluggishly over the slimy satin ribbons of the water-weeds.

One morning the three dogs and I walked aimlessly along the river bank until we came to a gully running inland from the water. I turned and walked up this, and ahead of me lay a coffee-coloured cow, right in the hot noonday sun. It was Corabelle, one of the prettiest of the milking herd; she lay there motionless, except for the swaying of her head which gave the impression of distress and suffering.

I called, 'Hullo, Corabelle!' and walked quietly towards her, telling the dogs to keep back. When I got near I could see the great dark eyes in her swaying head were full of pain. So I squatted beside her and rubbed her chocolate-dark forehead, saying, 'What's the matter, old girl?' There was no good shade near by, for the tall gum trees, with their pointed, grey-green leaves turned sideways to the sun, threw a mere dusting of shadowy confetti across the hard gold of the sunshine.

Something was very wrong with Corabelle; I rose to my feet and walked around her. Her creamy-coffee sides were pressed upwards by the earth, her body trembled and quivered. I touched her side, and the burning heat of the sun and the animal heat of the hide together troubled my palm. I came round to her head, and then I saw her near foreleg.

'Oh Cora – poor Cora, you're hurt!' I cried, and squatted down again and passed my hand over her delicately-carved, silken head in an effort to comfort her. I pulled off my old straw hat, but it looked small and silly between the cow's head and the sun, with all that great body burning and shuddering beyond it. Saliva dripped from the cow's mouth and now and again she made a low, mooing noise, full of sorrow. I put my hat on again and looked around for some way to shelter her. Even the dogs seemed to be feeling the heat, and lay panting in the sparse shade.

I knew that Corabelle must be dreadfully thirsty,

and I walked back towards the river, looking for something in which I could carry water. There was nothing. Close to the water's edge someone had left a rusty old fruit tin, but the cow could not get her muzzle into that. I dipped my hat into the water but it simply poured through.

Then I had a bright idea – Ben should take a message back to Lewis! I tore a strip from the hem of my cotton frock, and made some ink by puddling up a little water in the rusty tin. On the material I scratched a shaky 'S.O.S.', and with another strip I tied the message round Benny's neck, because, of course, the little dog could not run all that way without panting. He wriggled with eagerness, and I said:

'Take it to *Lewis* – to *Lewis* –' and off he galloped.

I was still puzzled how to get water to Corabelle when I stumbled across a patch of broad, green dock-leaves growing from the brown leaf-mould that edged the water, thickening every year when autumn came and the willows shed their leaves. I picked a big handful of dock-leaves, and squatting on the leaf-mould I pushed the stems and leaftips into the straw hat, and then added bits of the clay mud to make them stick down, twining leaves into all the crevices, until finally the crown of the hat had a thick, leafy lining. Then I gave it an experimental dip into the water. It leaked badly, of course, but if I carried the rusty fruit tin full of water as well as the hat it would give Cora a few cool sips.

I staggered up the bank, never raising my eyes from the diminishing water, and when I got to Corabelle the hat was still half full. I put it before her and stroked my wet hand across her muzzle, so that she would understand that this strange bucket held water. Cora put out her long tongue and drank thirstily. Then I jumped to my feet, meaning to refill the hat and the tin. I heard

Algy coming towards Cora and told him to go back. He gave a funny little whine and I looked up – imagine my terrific excitement; for the first time I noticed that Cora had twisted herself into a half circle, and there, lying near her on the sunburnt grass, small and wet and beautiful, lay a new-born calf!

It was a miracle of life, and I knelt before it and touched the little creature gently, while the helpless mother stirred her heavy body and tried to move nearer to her calf. I knew what she wanted, and put my arms round the honey-coloured mite and pushed it against its mother. The baby made a few weak little movements with its small head, dwarfed by the big ears of a baby animal, and looked at the world from great, liquid black eyes, then bent its head and started to drink.

I ran back to the river and brought more water, and when Cora had had enough I kept wetting her hot head with the cool water until I heard shouts in the distance. Then I stood up and ran up the bank, and there was my brave rescuer, Benny, galloping madly through the tall brown grass stems, with Lewis in hot pursuit, but still some way behind him. Benny sprang into my arms, thrilled with himself! He gasped and panted and his tongue hung out like a little piece of red flannel. Lewis called:

'What was the S.O.S. about?'

'It's Cora – Oh Lewis, I'm so glad you're here!'

Lewish went quietly to Cora's head and rubbed her ears.

'Now, old girl, let's see that leg –'

Poor Cora mooed unhappily; one look told him the leg was broken.

'We'll need help. We must build her a shelter here.'

'And the baby calf?'

'That'll be up to you, you can bring it up on the bottle.'

'Oh, I couldn't take it from Cora!'

Lewis looked worried: 'She can't do much for it, she'll have to lie here until her leg sets and be fed and watered where she is.'

'All right – I'll look after them both,' I said.

Then Lewis took his big sheath-knife and cut some forked branches, and rigged rather a shaky shelter over the cow and her calf. Then we went home to get splints for Cora's leg and other things. I was not allowed to return with the men, but Lewis said I could come along in an hour. When we got there Cora's leg, which had fortunately been broken low down, was set, and the shelter and fence were almost built. Cora had a heap of hay in front of her, and water within reach, the ceaseless, suffering movement of her head had stopped, and she no longer moaned.

We lifted the baby on to its trembling little legs and for a few moments it stood looking at us with its great eyes, then it folded up like some lovely velvet toy, and lay close to its mother again. I knew that ordinarily Cora would lick her calf tidily all over, and nudge it until it rose to its feet every now and again, so that it would soon be strong enough to get up and down easily; and Lewis told me that I must do Cora's work for her; get the calf up and down, and rub it down every day with a rubber sponge squeezed out of salty water.

Finally we left them both well provided for, and Algy, Ben and I scrambled into the truck with the others, while Ajax loped alongside, and we all went home.

My father came home from his trip next day, and as I was with Cora he walked up to see me. He put his hand on my shoulder and said:

'You're a good girl. But for you Cora would have died, so now it's only fair that she and her calf should belong to you!'

I was very excited, but I said:

'What about Benny – he did it really.'

'It wouldn't be much use giving them to Benny!'

'Anyway, I think we ought to make a fuss of him –'

'All right, we'll do just that, though I can't think of any extra fuss we *can* make, we can't give him more pocket-money!'

That night I was very happy as I lay in bed looking into the deep bush night that lay where the velvety-black stretched away from the verandah, and I thought of my beautiful cow and her calf. From the trees at the river's edge a hundred yards away came the soft 'ka ka kàkaka' of a possum; then the cry of a dingo, full of an infinite melancholy; and the sound I loved best of all, the sound that even now makes my heart turn over with homesickness, the surging sea-sound of a herd of weaners penned into the yards and calling to their mothers outside, their cries rising and falling, and filling the night air.

There was one more sound before I dropped off to sleep. Benny trotted to the verandah steps, and I saw his small back, black against the moonlight, as he raised his little nose high in the air and gave one long, quavering, miniature wolf-call. Then he trotted back, and jumped on my feet where he loved to sleep, and from where he took great pleasure in lording it over the other dogs.

12. Algy and the Stone Age Men

Always in the back of my mind ran the thought of the dread day when I would have to go to boarding school. Then, when Brownie came to us, and I enjoyed my lessons so much, the fear of something that grew nearer year by year, faded again. But just after Corabelle and her calf joined my own particular family, I overheard my mother and father and Brownie in a conversation that started me fretting once again over the thought of school, and the leaving behind of all the creatures I loved. I found that my parents were very worried because I had no other children to play with. I did not consciously miss other children, but they thought it was bad for me to be brought up in this solitary fashion, and they were considering sending me off to boarding school instead of waiting until I was fifteen, as they had always meant to do. The thought of this seemed to bring the separation from my dear dogs very near to me; I heard my father say:

'The child simply adores the new calf,' and my mother answered: 'I know, it does worry me. Every new animal means another tie for her to break when she goes to school, and she is going to be so dreadfully unhappy, I do feel that, for her own sake, we should send her soon now.'

I could not listen any more, I called the dogs and we went wandering through the bush until I was very tired, and then we came home and I went silently to bed, refusing my tea, and my mother came to my bed and inquired anxiously if I were ill. I could not tell her what troubled me; like all bush creatures I had learnt to keep my fears to myself, and it was long after she left me that I went to sleep. Then, later that night, something happened that drove all thought of school out of everyone's minds for many months, and gave us a new and wonderful experience, even though it was rather terrifying at the time.

Early in the morning hours I woke up to find the dogs whining and pawing at my bed. Smoke drifted through the night air, there was a great crackling noise, men shouted, and the tall gum trees along the river bank were lit by a brilliant, flickering light. Then my mother and one of the station hands came to my bed, rolled me in a blanket and carried me, still half-asleep, off the verandah and away from the house, with the dogs running alongside.

Fire had broken out, one end of the long house was blazing, and the kitchen was already a mass of flames and charred wood. There was a stiff breeze blowing, and it was all the men could do to beat the flames back from the rest of the house.

The result of this fire was that after a lot of talking it was decided that my parents and I would go for the next few months to our other station, Gulaggi, which was on the fringe of the Central Australian desert; and that Brownie should have a long holiday. My mother and I had never been to Gulaggi, it had always been considered too primitive, and too difficult a journey for us; but we both had always wanted to go, because round there was the really primitive life of Australia, and it was the last stronghold of the wild Myall blacks.

This journey should have made both Ajax and Benny more humble if they had only realized it. For Ajax, the kingly, aloof dog with the golden beauty of ripe corn, and Benny, the naughty little show-off, meant very little to the Myalls, who looked upon Algy, humble, sweetly-stupid Algy, as a god. The Myalls had never seen a bulldog before, and so he seemed a god to them. Ajax was a devil, and Benny, who considered himself a vastly superior type to the other two, was to the Myalls not even a very good snack, and I am sure he would have ended up in a cooking-pot if I had not watched him every minute. He would have been so angry if he had known why the Myalls took the slightest interest in him!

My parents decided to make the long journey in the truck, and to take the dogs as we always did. Much of the trip was through wild bush country, with tracks but no roads, and we had to take lots of spares for the cars, food and water, mosquito nets and goodness knows what else, for the journey took weeks.

Finally we started, and let the dogs out every few hours; they ran after the slowly-moving truck, Algy puffing and blowing and getting picked up first, then Benny, and lastly the tireless Ajax. During the last part of the trip we touched the fringe of the desert, where the air was so hot and dry that it burned and the vivid blue of the sky hurt the eyes. Around us grew the drab spinifex bushes, mulga, mallee and currajong trees. Once we passed what seemed to be miles of scarlet carpet, but which was really the beautiful, brilliant desert pea. Then we met our first camel train, twelve of the queer, awkward creatures, swaying along with their ungainly walk, prodded by their Afghan driver, snaking their long necks and grumbling and snarling bad-temperedly to themselves the whole time.

Insects and mosquitoes were very troublesome, and I wore long blue overalls. These later completely foxed the Aborigines, who never could decide whether I was a little girl in boys' pants, or a little boy with long hair!

We found Gulaggi homestead much smaller than

Gunyan, and with a mosquito net-screened verandah running all around it. Central Australia is a strange, dry country; where scattered showers fall there may be patches of moist green grass, as well as flowering shrubs and bright quandong and acacia trees, but for the most part it looks, I think, rather like the lunar landscape will look to the first man who reaches the moon – a vast, strange land of subdued colours, dry and crumbling. Here and there are small hidden water-holes, or the dry shine of salt-encrusted lakes, and endless plains out of which great rocky formations rise abruptly, like colossal natural cathedrals with rounded roofs.

In this sparse and rather terrible land live the scattered tribes of Aborigines, usually called Myalls, I suppose, from the skimpy scrubs that give them shelter. These stringy, muscular warriors hunt with spears of their own make, and they are so black that they have the purplish tinge of a mulberry. They wander about the trackless land, for ever searching for food, eating anything they can capture or spear, iguanas, birds, desert rats, emus, wild camels, or digging the yams which grow in patches in the hard earth, and which taste like sweet potatoes. They live just as their ancestors lived, the Stone Age men of countless thousands of years ago. For water they have only their 'soaks', muddy little water-holes which they keep carefully hidden, and which have been known to their tribes from time immemorial. These 'soaks' mean life itself to the black men, who often travel a hundred miles between them in their never-ending search for food.

It was probably the travellers' tales told so often to my father that decided him to make a trip south to see the amazing Ayers Rock, which rises straight from the plains to a height of a thousand feet, and is about two miles long and a mile broad. My mother did not want to go on the long and difficult trip, but my father agreed to take me, and, of course, the dogs. Jim, an old bushman near us who had been in this land for forty years and could talk to the Abos, decided to join us. He was a great friend of mine, and knew a great deal about this strange life around us. Jim had a wonderful collection of the Abos' work, their canoe-shaped wooden 'pitchis', in which they carry food; their spears and wommeras, the sticks which they use for launching their spears; and he even had a pair of the rare 'kaditcha' shoes, which are worn only by medicine men and are very sacred. They are made of emu feathers stuck together with human blood, and even the miraculous black trackers cannot tell which way a man is walking when he has them on. The Abos say that when a man wears the kaditcha shoes he becomes endowed with supernatural powers.

I was delighted that Jim was to be in our party; he loved the dogs and they loved him, so of course he could do no wrong in my eyes. The first day of the trip we had two punctures, but these things came as a matter of course; the heat and the dry, thorny things that come out of spinifex are very hard on tyres.

We often saw willy-willys circling about the endless bare lands. A willy-willy is a sort of whirlwind that looks like a thin brown column of smoke dancing across the plain; when one is near you it looks like a spinning cone, its centre a vortex of wind and sand and anything else the willy-willy picks up on its mad journey. We were having our lunch one day, sitting on the side of the truck in the shade, when a willy-willy raced towards us, and before we could scramble out of the way it hit us! It whirled Ben away several yards and filled our food with sand. It took us about an hour to collect our scattered utensils, and to get what sand we could out of our clothes and Ben's coat. Benny was most indignant about the whole thing; I am sure he thought it was a silly trick we had played on him, and he snarled and grumbled for ages after the willy-willy was far away.

Now and again we would see about a dozen desert men standing on hilltops, or peering from among the dried grasses of the plain, their lubras, which is what they call their women, standing behind them carrying the tiny piccaninnies that were too small to walk, or else holding their firesticks, long pliant branches bound together at the top, decorated by knobs of brilliant red from the shiny seeds of some desert plant. The naked children peered through matted hair decorated by a sort of shaggy fringe that went all around the head, weighted down by brown seed-pods about as big as grapes.

The dogs were always restless when the Abos were about, and I used to keep them close to me, especially Ben, after Jim warned me that the Abos would love to eat him! Sometimes we saw piccaninnies with the most extraordinarily distended tummies, and Jim said this was because they, like the camels, filled themselves up at water-holes, drinking until they could hold no more, because the water had to last them until they reached the next hole.

One day I found Algy almost standing on his head, as he did when he wanted to sniff at anything on the ground, so I looked, and found he was peering at a fat, legless, ant-creature. I scooped it up on a piece of bark and took it back to Jim, who told me it was a parasite ant, one of a tribe of desert ants with the unpleasant habit of biting the legs off a few of their brothers. They then stuffed the helpless ants with food until they got rolling fat, then during the hard winter the rest of the ants ate those living storehouses.

Later on, Algy and Ben were both delighted with

themselves when they dug out another sort of these cannibal ants. These were called 'honey ants', and they stuffed members of their tribe with honey as reservoirs for hard times. The dogs found the fat, helpless, honey-filled creatures delicious, but I must say I thought it revolting of them.

One day Jim talked with a desert warrior he knew, a big, gaunt man, with a plait of grass round his forehead to tie his shaggy hair back, and carrying a narrow wooden shield and a long barbed spear. Jim learned that the tribe were having a corroboree that night, on a sacred ground not far from our camp. The warrior chief agreed that we might see it, on condition that we kept very quiet, the dogs were left behind, and the 'boy' – that was I – kept quiet and stood behind the two men. When the moon rose we shut our dogs in the back of the car, and walked quietly to a little rise overlooking the ground, where we were almost hidden by grass and bushes. We could hear the Abos before we reached the rise, making strange, savage, chanting noises, and when we were in sight it was a savage picture too. The Myalls, their bodies shining with grease and banded in ochre and white, were rattling their spears and wommeras, and stamping their feet in savage rhythm. They had bunches of dried grass thrust through their nostrils, like moustaches that were growing too high up, and round their heads were strips of furry hide and grass to hold back their wild, matted locks.

I watched entranced; no women were allowed on the sacred corroboree grounds, and the lubras squatted in the background, nursing their piccaninnies and keeping their backs to the dancing warriors. After a time the painted, weaving bodies, the steady stamping and hoarse cries seemed to mesmerize me, and the next thing I knew was that Jim was carrying me back to the car!

'You're a fine one to fall asleep when I take you to a party!' he laughed, and I *was* annoyed with myself, I knew I would probably never see another corroboree just like that one – and I never have.

We were about a day away from Ayers Rock, with the dogs out of the car and having a run, when we heard the rare sound of Ajax's deep bark. My father stopped the car and we went towards the sound. Ajax was standing over the figure of a man, an Abo lying in the dry grass. Jim rolled him over; he was an old man, and unconscious.

'Thirst!' Jim said, and put his finger into the man's mouth and hooked out a stone. Blacks carry stones in their mouths to help them keep down their thirst. The men carried the old fellow back to the car and gave him a little water, and presently he came to, and Jim told him that Ajax had found him. With the great toughness of these Stone Age men, he soon recovered and was as good as new. It seemed he had some sort of accident, and, as they always must, the tribe, which was on a migration from one soak to another, had left him.

The old chap was delighted with the food and drink we gave him, and seemed most grateful in his own way. We put down a piece of tarpaulin for him to sleep on, but in the morning he was gone. The next morning, in the dawn sunlight before us, the great Ayers Rock rose like a tower of shimmering gold. No wonder it was a sort of sacred temple to the Abos, who knew all the huge, red-walled caverns high up its sides, on the walls of which their ancestors had drawn bats and birds, and strange, ghostly figures.

On the horizon was the thin, wavering spire of bluish 'talk' smoke, for the Abo, like the Indian, uses coloured smoke made by different plants to talk from one tribe to another. We were to camp near a waterhole at one end of the Rock. Around the hole the skimpy trees were filled with small, screeching parrots, and a species of doves with plumage of softest blue. And there, standing beside the water-hole, was a baby emu, the dearest little thing with a three-cornered face, and wearing what looked like a jumper of brown and black stripes. It was not a bit afraid, and Algy and I wanted to adopt it, but Jim said it would be better back with its mother, and presently it wandered off.

Just as we pulled up another tyre went, and while the men were working on it the dogs and I started up the face of the Rock. It was terribly hot, but I climbed on and on, with the dogs struggling and panting beside me. Presently we landed into one of the big, bare caves that honeycomb the rock. Ajax loped out of sight through the open end of the cave, and suddenly I felt far away from everyone and rather frightened. I told myself not to be silly, and that it would be stupid to go back without exploring. Ben was still with me, but Algy had disappeared. I called, the echoes came back to me but not the dogs. Then Ben gave a yap and pelted off to the end of the cave and disappeared. I waited a while, calling him, and looking at the scrawled drawings on the walls.

Then I got panicky, and ran to where the dogs had disappeared. I found myself in a boulder-strewn passage which was very dark. I felt my way along, and then suddenly my foot slipped on the loose stones and I felt myself falling, clawing and scrabbling at the loose rocks and sand that fell with me. I must have fallen fifteen feet or more when I came to a slithering stop and stood up. I looked around me, and I knew real terror!

I was in a great, red-walled cave. All around the walls were scrawled aboriginal drawings, men and beasts made from single strokes of some sort of ochre and brown pigment. Then I heard Ben's familiar yap, and I looked across the cave to where, still and silent, a dozen gaunt, wild-looking warriors stood. In the centre of them was Algy, panting heavily, and looking very bewildered and embarrassed. Round his neck was a noose of plaited grass. In front of him squatted an evil figure that I knew must be the medicine man, for at his side was the little 'dillybag', or leather pouch in which medicine men keep such 'sacred' objects as bits of human bone, strands of hair, dried lizards and so forth; and in front of him lay Ben, Ben, with his little legs tied together with grass rope, his red tongue panting, and every now and again yelping with indignation. Around this group was drawn a circular line of white. I remembered what Jim had said about Benny making a nice tit-bit for an Abo's supper!

Algy tried to come to me, he wriggled and twisted and the grass noose tightened, but it would not give. The warriors stopped moving about and stood absolutely still, obviously taken aback by my sudden entrance. I moved towards the group, and two of the warriors stepped between me and the dogs, and stood immovable. I could only think of one thing to do, so I raised my voice and called despairingly:

'Ajax! Ajax!'

For an instant everything was still, then there was a rush of feet and Ajax bounded through the opening behind the warriors, leaped across Algy and reached my side, turning to face the men, his hackles erect, his eyes a warning red, and that terrible slow thunder vibrating in his chest.

The medicine man scrambled back from Ben, who yelped and struggled harder than ever, and Algy stood still and gazed beseechingly at Ajax and me. I put my hand on Ajax's shoulder, and, stiff-legged and menacing, he stepped forward, while I tried not to look frightened and shivered with terror inside. Again we moved a step forward, and I thought that the warriors did not look quite so confident; certainly the medicine man was upset; he scrabbled about in the dust of the ring gabbling to himself. We moved forward again – and through the opening ahead of us came another black figure.

There was something familiar about this man, but I was not sure what it was. He stepped forward and squatted down in the circle, facing the first medicine man, and the newcomer threw his dillybag down by his side. It was clear that the first man just did not not know what to do; and the warriors, instead of standing with that dreadful stillness, began to move and mutter among themselves. Ben had stopped yapping, he just whimpered a little, which broke my heart, but I dared not move towards him until I was sure what the new man was up to. There was much talk and shouting, then the second man's voice rose angrily, the first man threw his arm across his eyes and scurried backwards like some great black crab, and when he was outside the white circle he rose to his feet and ran through the gap in the wall.

The second medicine man rose to his feet and beckoned to me; I was still afraid but I knew that I must not show it, and Ajax and I walked forward together. Then I knew who the man was! He was the Abo we had rescued two nights before – I called out to him and he smiled and nodded his head. The rest of the warriors simply melted away through the dark hole at the back of the cave. I ran forward and untied Algy and Benny, and hugged them with relief and happiness. Finally the old man led the way down the cliffside, and we arrived back at the car, and I told my father what had happened, and the old man talked to Jim.

I went over to them and thanked him for saving us.

We gave him some tins out of our food-store, but this did not seem enough for all he had done for me, so I took off the gold bangle I always wore and gave it to him, because it was the best thing I had. He seemed very pleased, and I knew it would be a strong 'medicine' with the tribe; then he walked away round the Rock.

Jim said that the warriors I had seen in the cave had followed us across country, using their own short cuts, because they had never seen any dog like Algy, and if they had been able to they would have kidnapped him long before because they believed he must be a very powerful god. But they were afraid of Ajax, they believed *he* was a demon. When they caught, silly, friendly old Algy in the cave, and trapped Ben, they did not anticipate that I would fall in from the roof. If I had not come along they would have sacrificed Ben to Algy! But I appeared and called up the demon Ajax, and that made them doubt the power of their medicine man.

Even so, it might have ended tragically if the Myall we had rescued had not in his turn rescued us. Having met the great god Algy socially, so to speak, as well as the demon Ajax, who had saved his life, he felt he owed us all something, and he certainly more than paid his debt.

13. The Cave Diggers

When we returned to Gulaggi from Ayers Rock we had another two months to stay, before it was arranged that we should return to Gunyan in time for my brother's long Christmas holidays. Although the fire had put off talk about my going to boarding school, I had a nasty feeling that it would be revived once I was home again. However, when we returned to Gunyan in due time, and found Brownie waiting for us, I forgot my worry in the joy of playing with Matilda, and the excited, loving welcome of Kiko and Possy. And then my brother arrived and he and I were together most of the time, riding, playing tennis and fishing through the long summer days.

One day we decided to dig a cave in the side of one of the few high banks that faced the river where it curved round the house. My brother liked to do things in a big way, so we set to work digging with a perfect fury that seemed to infect the dogs, and they began to dig furiously too – for a few minutes, until they got tired of the idea! Benny was always scrambling through our legs and putting in his twopennorth, which really was not much help from such a little fellow; but Ajax scooped out quite a lot of damp earth with his huge paws, and we would sit back on our heels and let him go at it. Algy could have been quite useful too, but he would dig for a moment, and then be so fascinated by the things he turned up, the wood beetles and earthworms and other wriggly creatures that love wet earth, that he would stop digging and begin to sniff and snuff at whatever was wriggling about, snorting and barking when it tickled his nose – he would never have gone very far as a miner, I am afraid!

We were so pleased with what we were doing that we often stayed the whole day on the river bank, taking a picnic lunch, and splashing about in the cool water when we got too hot for words. When we were asked what we were doing, we simply said 'digging a cave', and nobody bothered any more.

When we were very tired we would scramble down the bank and sit by a submerged log watching for the pale, ghostly shrimps to come walking along it on their threadlike legs. We collected some planks from Lewis, and used them to shore up the crumbling sides of the cave, making rather a wobbly job of it. One day my father came down as we were making billy tea on the little beach below the cave. We invited him to climb up the bank and take a look at our cave, but he only laughed and refused. Obviously he thought we had some tiny hole in the bank, and my brother and I looked at each other and did not say any more, making up our minds that as soon as it was big enough we would invite both parents to tea *in* the cave!

So we went on digging and battering planks into position, in between swims in which the dogs joined. One day Algy was paddling and snorting about the edge of the water when he yelped suddenly; we rushed towards him, he threw his head up, and to our horror something long and leathery and black was attached to the roll of flesh just behind the black button of his nose. The poor old boy was terrified, and so were we; he dashed about shaking his head, the thing clung on, and then we realized that it was not a snake but a big black horse leech – a horrid creature but not dangerous.

Algy calmed down after a bit, for leeches do not hurt at all, and when nothing worse happened than the flapping of the nasty thing about his face, he squatted on his haunches, shook his head, and tried to peer at it, first with one eye and then with the other. All the time the leech grew fatter, until at last it simply dropped off. Then Algy bounded backwards as it lay there on the sand, gorged and horrible but quite harmless. Algy gave a few snorts and half-hearted grabs at it until Benny noticed him. Then Benny, behaving like a Lord Mayor who is keeping a procession waiting, bounced up barking loudly, seized the thing in his little jaws, and flung it into the air. Finally he flung it into the water and the portly leech floated away. Then you could almost see Benny dusting the palms of his front paws and saying: 'There! *I* fixed that!' as he trotted away on some other all-important business that needed his attention!

As we dug deeper into the bank the work went more slowly. We stamped all the earth we had dug out into quite a little platform outside the cave entrance. Then we decided that we couldn't wait for the day when we would have the cave eight feet into the bank and five feet high, but, as we were half-way, we would give a preliminary house-warming. So we gave up work for that day and went down on the beach and built a 'volcano'. The volcano was a big mound of earth and sand, damped and patted down until it was very firm. Then, as gently as possible, we tunnelled from opposite sides, and the dogs were not allowed to help! When the tunnel was through and the centre widened a little, we ran a straight, pointed stick from the peaked top to the lower chamber. This was the tricky part, for the whole thing might collapse. Once safely through this, it was time to search for kindling, tiny bits of dry wood or anything else that would make a good smoke. This was

The dogs began to dig furiously also.

worked carefully into the middle hollow, and we lit it with the blazing end of a dry stick. When the kindling caught, the smoke poured out of the hole at the top, and we sat around feeding the internal fires with tiny twigs – until we got tired of it.

We issued formal invitations to our parents, Brownie and Lewis for one Saturday afternoon, and with much heaving and pushing we managed to get quite a thick log into position on the platform outside the cave, as we knew that grown-ups did not think highly of sitting on the ground. We nailed slats across an old garden stool to make a table, and put scraps of carpet on the damp floor. A small wooden box held the tea-cups, and I put a mass of wattle blossom into tins and jars inside the cave. This made both of us and the dogs sneeze violently. Benny went further than sneezing, he shoved his curious little nose into a thick clump of the golden blossoms, and got stung on the tip of it by a bee that had refused to pick up its pollen plus fours and fly away!

It was a hot afternoon as we waited for our guests, and we looked longingly where the river sparkled like silver paper in the sunlight, and lay cool as grey glass in the shade of the willows. Benny had a blue bow round his neck which he rather enjoyed, and he galloped down the bank and took an admiring peek at himself in the still, willow-fringed pools every once in a while.

Everything was ready, billy boiling, sticky cakes wheedled out of the cook and covered by a tin plate to keep the flies off, when our guests arrived, hot and panting from their scramble up the steep bank. I thought my mother and Brownie behaved in the way guests should, but my father and Lewis behaved rather strangely as we gestured proudly towards the cave, and they saw it for the first time. Feeling that they were not as impressed as they should have been, we hastened to explain that it was only half finished, and that we were going to dig at least twice as far into the bank before we stopped – then maybe we would camp right *in* the cave for the rest of the holidays!

Our father remarked feebly that we must have worked very hard. Lewis doubled his six feet into half and went into the cave and examined the shoring-up boards, then came out and said defensively:

'I gave them the boards, boss, but I didn't know they wanted them for *this*!'

'But we told you we were building a cave!' I said. We were a little disappointed at the lack of enthusiasm, but put it down to the silly way grown-ups often went on; then we ate a whopping tea ourselves, saw our guests off, tidied up and had a swim before we went home.

When we were in bed on the mosquito-netted verandah, our father came to say good night. He looked a little upset, and we soon found out why.

'I blame myself for not looking at the cave when you invited me, but – well, you know how busy I am. I had no idea your cave was in the curve of the bank that guides the water away from the homestead, nor that it was so big. It would be very dangerous to have that great hole there in flood time, so I'll have to disappoint you and ask you not to go on with the digging –'

At this stage I burst into loud wailings; now my brother would treat me like a baby again and I just could not bear it! At my wails the three dogs leaped on to the bed, or rather Benny and Algy did, nearly smothering me with their loving kisses, while Ajax stood with his front feet on the bed, towering over me, anxious-eyed and loving, growling at the invisible enemy he thought must be menacing me.

When everyone had calmed down a little, we both realized that our father was right, we just had not thought about the terrible floods that occasionally swept down on the homestead, like the one in which I had found Ajax. Next day Lewis examined the planks supporting the cave and said that we must not go in it again, because it might collapse any minute.

So we were forbidden our cave, and it was left for the planks to be removed, and the earth to be filled in, some time when there were men to spare for the job. But on a station there never *are* men to spare for anything, and so the cave stayed as it was.

When my brother went back to school I missed him dreadfully. It had been lovely to have my own brother to play with, and I tried hard to keep up with his much more grown-up idea of games, taking all sorts of risks, and being frightened to death half the time by the things he expected me to be able to do.

Then one day after he had returned to school I suddenly felt very lonely for him, and thought I would just *look* at the cave again, and remember the happy time we had had digging it. Of course I would not go in – I would just *look*. So the dogs and I scrambled up the familiar bank, and found the cave looking much the same, only rather dilapidated where there had been little falls of earth, or where the planks had buckled out from the sides. Then I felt I *must* crawl into it, just once, for old times' sake; so in I went with Benny in front, Algy just behind me, and Ajax standing in the entrance. We three rather crowded it, and we bumped against the boards as we got to the end, and were turning round to get out again.

Then it happened. Suddenly a shower of earth fell on us all. Benny turned and bolted out, but Algy was bigger and slower. I tried to hurry him out, for I was covered in a film of earth and half blinded by it, and really terrified by the creaking, buckling noises from the wooden supports. In my fluster I noticed that Algy's hind-quarters were in front of me as I turned towards the opening, and that I couldn't see his big head and shoulders, and there was only a gap of less than eighteen inches facing me. I got down on my stomach and wriggled through this, and then to my horror I saw that the wooden props had fallen across Algy's shoulders, and earth from the top of the cave had fallen too, so that Algy was pinned there. Only his strong front legs allowed him to keep the space free for me to crawl through, and now I was beyond him. I could see his distress. He was panting and could not move; if his front legs gave way and released more debris he would be crushed.

I did not know what to do, for I could see that he could not stand the pressure on his back for long. I tried frantically to find something with which to lever the load up, but there was nothing. In despair I stood for an instant trying to think of something and then I heard the sound of horses' hooves on the shingle of the river crossing below us. I turned towards the sound and saw two of the stockmen riding towards me, the reins loose on the necks of their tired horses. I stood still and screamed:

'Help! Help!'

The men looked up and saw me. I yelled again, and they came galloping towards me, splashing through the shallow, glittering water of the ford. By now I was yelling and sobbing together:

'Hurry – oh, do hurry! It's Algy – oh, hurry, help him!'

They jumped off their horses and came scrambling up the bank, and I pushed them towards the mouth of the cave. They could see in an instant what was happening to my Algy, and they rolled the stump we had put outside for a seat right into the gap beside Algy, then they managed to get a board from the mouth of the cave and to lever up the mass of earth and boards off Algy's back. Poor fellow, he staggered out panting, his legs trembling, and threw himself down outside.

'Phew! That was a near thing!' one of the men said. 'Let the old chap rest a minute, then we'll take you home.'

The men squatted on their heels and lit cigarettes, and when Algy had recovered we all went home. I would have felt happier about this adventure if my father had insisted on a definite punishment for my disobedience, but he did not. Had he known it, he did something far worse; he looked at my mother in a worried way and said:

'That settles it, Jean. That child is like a wild animal, and she's always in danger of one sort or the other. She should be living like any other little girl, playing with children of her own age at *safe* games. Don't you see, she really should go to boarding school. Do make up your mind to it, and get her ready to go to Armidale after the mid-winter term.'

That was punishment indeed.

14. Homemade Circus

Birthdays were great events in our family, and because my brother's birthday fell on a day of his Easter holidays it was arranged that he should come home for that fortnight, instead of staying somewhere near the school as he usually did, except for the long, twice-yearly holidays, when he always came home.

Actually his birthday fell on the day before he had to leave on his return to school, but that gave us nearly two weeks in which to plan some sort of party. The day after he reached home we walked up to the big round yard together. It was about a quarter of a mile from the homestead, and in the yard, which was shaded by a couple of rough-barked wild apple trees, lived a great Clydesdale stallion. Its huge hooves were topped from knee to fetlock in what looked like ballet skirts of long hair, and its mane tossed from side to side from the fleshy crest that rose in a proud curve on the massive neck – it was a wonderful creature that looked as if it should be carrying a knight heavy with shining armour and a long jousting pole, such as only a powerful man on a giant horse could carry.

We watched the big draught thunder about the yards from where we perched on the top rail of the fence, and then the dogs followed us up a short ladder to the loft of the little building belonging to the yard, and the hay made us a comfortable couch. The dogs climbed ladders as well as we did, and Benny was a great tree climber, and used to follow us up sloping trunks and along the lower branches, more like a cat than a little dog.

We lay there, panting with heat. The wooden doors left at least a twelve-foot gap where they were pushed back for greater coolness, and we watched the heavy stallion kick and squeal as a horse-fly bit him on the rump. We laughed, and Garth said:

'It's just like a seat at the circus, sitting here and watching old Magnificence the Third kicking up his heels . . . I say! How about a circus for my birthday?'

'Oh *yes*! But how –?'

'It'd be easy. Lewis'd help, one of us could be ring-master while the other performed – and look –' he jumped to his feet, 'we'd push the hay back and put a bench up here for the audience. *You* ought to be pretty good, think of the circus performance you and the dogs gave at the Inverell Show last year!'

This really wasn't fair – it was not my fault that the dogs went on as they did. I had been upset at the time, but now I could laugh at it with my brother, as we looked back on it, and planned our own circus.

That dreadful Inverell Show fiasco had happened because my father felt that my beautiful mare Belle was ready for the show-ring. She was under fourteen hands high, which is the right height for a polo pony, and she was a bright chestnut with tiny brown flecks that you could only see when you rubbed her hide upwards. I was proud of those flecks because they were said to belong only to descendants of the great horse Carbine, and his stock was coveted by all horse-lovers.

We always stayed with friends, the Andersens, in Inverell, because they had a big garden and loved to have the dogs. When we arrived for the show I was rather upset, because the Andersens, thinking it would be a nice surprise for me, had entered Algy in the show, where his rivals were limited to one local bulldog! I would never enter any of the dogs in shows because I knew that they would hate it, but I felt I could not hurt the Andersens' feelings by refusing to show Algy, so I just made up my mind to make the whole thing as easy and pleasant for him as I could manage. None of my dogs were fit to be show dogs; they had never been tied up, or had even worn collars. Ajax would stalk at heel anywhere, but Algy and Benny simply had not a clue on how to behave in the street.

We went to the showground and inspected the dogs' pavilion, which was very nice, fitted with rows of wooden kennels, each one a gaily-painted little house with a peaked roof, open in front, and with a chain attached to the side of the door. We met an official who was most interested in Ajax; indeed, wherever I went people stared at him. I told the official how it came about that I was showing Algy, and he was most sympathetic, and said I could tie Benny up with Algy, and put Ajax in the kennel next door, so that Algy would have his own friends with him.

When the opening day arrived I was so upset about leaving Algy that I lost interest in my own events. I got into my riding clothes, and then we took the dogs to the show-ring. I made a big sacrifice to soften Algy's hard lot, and wrapped my party dress in a piece of paper and took it with us. It was a sapphire-blue velveteen, and Algy loved rubbing his face on it, so I thought it would comfort him to have it in his kennel, and I spread it well inside on the clean dry straw.

That evening my mother was amazed that she had left my frock behind, and sure that she remembered packing it!

The first day passed uneventfully, and Belle won the first heat for the best polo pony, and came third in the ladies' hacks. My mother stayed with the dogs while I was in the ring, but I was with them the rest of the time, and Benny got very tired of being carried about, because whenever I put him down he got into some trouble or other. Algy's rival was a fine, fawn-coloured bulldog, used to shows, and to being handled by strangers and to being tied up. It was absurd to pit my old fellow against him. Dear Algy, he had not a notion of how to behave while he was being judged, and wagged his tail, sat down, and tried to lick the judge's hands all the time, so of course he did *not* win the prize; but as he was the only other bulldog entered they had to give him the second prize!

When the judging was over I patted Algy, told him how clever he was, and tied Benny beside him, had a word with Ajax next door, and rushed off to the ring to ride Belle in the polo pony finals. That was the first time all three dogs had been tied and left without any of their friends near them. Opposite Algy his rival sat, handsome in his blue ribbon. Algy hated *his* ribbon, so I tied it to his peaked roof.

Belle won the first prize in her class, and I hurried back to collect the boys. As I neared the pavilion I heard the most awful row going on, and a crowd milled about outside. I wormed my way in, deafened by those frightful snarling, roaring savage sounds with which dogs always fight. I knew without looking that Algy's weakness for a fight had been too much for him, but I was not prepared for the sight that greeted me. Inside the hall I found the crowd pressed back against the wall, and in the centre it looked as if several giant tortoises with brightly-painted peaked shells had gone mad and were charging at each other, making fearful wooden bangings and splintering sounds to add to the noise of the dogs.

Algy had suddenly decided that he hated his rival, just about at the moment his rival had come to the same conclusion, and they charged across the floor dragging their houses after them. Ben, bursting with excitement and chained to Algy's house was dragged along too, and added to the confusion by nipping both dogs, although I am sure he thought he was helping Algy, and he bounced backwards and forwards, trying to avoid having the kennel dragged over him!

At first Ajax looked on in his lordly way, but when officials rushed forward and tried to separate the dogs Ajax decided this move was directed against Algy, and he gave one of his great roars and dragged *his* house into the scrum, chasing the officials and everyone else back against the walls.

There he was when I came in, raging backwards and forwards, his house bumping madly after him like a cockle-shell, while behind him Algy and the blue-ribbon boy fought it out, tangling their chains, stamping on Benny and pulling their houses on top of themselves. Fortunately the chains held, so when I called Ajax to me and slipped his collar off the officials caught hold of the other houses and parted the dogs by sheer weight.

What a mess they were, panting and snarling and bitten all over, but not deeply. The champion's ribbon was just a mess – and my velveteen dress ...! Algy's red ribbon still waved gaily from the peak of his house. I got Benny undone; he was unhurt but filthy, covered in the big dogs' slather. The owner of the champion was as worried as I was, and kept apologizing to me. I was pretty sure that I should have been apologizing for Algy, but the mischief was done, so I let him take what credit he could for being the attacked and not the attacking one.

This was what my brother meant when he teased me about my circus act, but I told him he could not expect the dogs and me to do anything as spectacular as our show act over again. We decided to ask our father if we could move the stallion somewhere else for the time we needed to prepare the ring, and mother said we could have the birthday party in the room below the loft. Then we went into a huddle and thought out the acts. Of course Algy, Benny, Ajax, Matilda and Kiko had to be in it, but we let Possy off because he was always so sleepy in the daytime. Then there was Buck, my fat pony, Lewis's cattle dog, and my carpet snake Kaa. Kaa was beautifully marked and about nine feet long. He lived in a hole under the meathouse and kept the rats away. He was a fat, gentle creature, and seemed to like my pulling him about.

Then my brother did something that nearly wrecked the circus. My parents had a friend, a very nervous old lady, who used to visit us every now and again. Poor Mrs Carter, she was frightened of the dogs, never walked in the garden without keeping a nervous eye on Matilda, and nearly had a fit when Possy paid her a courtesy visit and sat on the end of her bed making faces and giving his soft 'ka kakakaa' noises. Even Kiko, that smallest and gentlest of monkeys, frightened her, and the mere suggestion of Kaa threw her into a frightful tizzy. I expect our parents thought she went on in a silly, exaggerated way, but they were fond of her, and so, in a way, were we, but we could not help teasing her sometimes. Mother made us promise that we would *never* bring Kaa into any of the little jokes we played on her, because she would most certainly have hysterics.

Mrs Carter walked about the garden, looking nervously in all directions, and one day she wandered towards one end of the garden where Garth had dug a big hole, which he called his 'mine'. Down there he would let off bunches of those red Chinese crackers, blasting, he called it. He was really a kind boy, but he simply could not resist playing jokes on Mrs Carter, so when she neared his mine he hopped down it and hid there, giving some mysterious hollow groans, and when the old lady peered nervously into the hole he let off a bunch of crackers! Mrs Carter leapt into the air with a squeal, and then of course she was furious and refused to speak to him, and went huffily back into the house and told our father. Then Father was very angry, and said that we could not have our circus. I cried, and he relented, because after all I had not done anything. Poor Garth was very upset; then Mrs Carter forgave him and, anxious to show her how sorry he was, he insisted on making her the guest of honour at his birthday circus, and the old lady was most flattered.

A few days before the circus, we took the Clydesdale out of the yard, and pushed the hay back in the loft so as to put a bench in front of the open loft doors. Then we tidied away the horse rugs and other paraphernalia downstairs, and put up a trestle table and folding chairs for the guests to sit on. We wondered how we were going to get Mrs Carter up the little ladder to the loft, and Garth said she would be sure to shut herself up in the folding chairs. Then he decided that, as guest of honour, Mrs Carter must have a special chair; so he borrowed a wheelbarrow and trundled it up to the yard with a wicker armchair and cushions in it. He was hot and tired when he got there, but he had that smug look people get when they feel that whatever they have done in the past has been atoned for. He put the chair at the top of the table, settled the cushions with proud pats, and that was that – or so he thought.

We were up early on the day of the circus. All the performers had to be in the yard, and Benny had two baths, because he promptly went out and rolled in something smelly after the first one and had to be bathed again. Algy had to be fished out from under the bed and dragged to the tub, where he stood like an outraged martyr while I scrubbed the padded wrinkles of his blessed bulldog face with a soft old tooth-brush. He always behaved as if he thought that a bath was a booby trap that would be sure to go off when he got in it! But once the deed was done he rather liked himself. Ajax was so big that I had to wash him in two sections, first with his front half in the tub, and then with his back half.

Buck was as groomed as his shaggy little body would allow, even Matilda was brushed. Kiko did not need touching, he was always sweet and clean, and I rubbed an oily rag over Kaa's beautifully-patterned coils until he was quite a dandy, though a very sleepy one. I could not lift him straight off the ground, but had to drape him round my shoulders and then lift the rest of him. I staggered up to the yard with him festooned about me, and looked around for somewhere to park him until it was time to take him into the ring to do his act with me – and I only hoped that, as my parents would be taking it quite calmly Mrs Carter would not have a fit. There was an old tree-stump just outside the yard, filled with crumbled bark and earth, and sprouting a few leafy twigs for shade, and that seemed a good place to put the sleepy, full-fed Kaa. I curled him round carefully, glad to be rid of his weight, and then left him in peace while I went back for Matilda.

The audience in the dress circle numbered six: Mrs Carter, our parents, Nessie, once our nurse and now the housekeeper, Brownie, and the bookkeeper, a young man who was almost as nervous of us as Mrs Carter was. Lewis, of course, was to help us in the ring.

Benny had a large bow on his neck, and after a few wild moments of trying to chew it off he seemed to take to it, and kept peering back at the ends of the bow to make sure it was there. I had made clown's caps and ruffs for Ajax and Algy out of crinkled paper. First I dressed the bewildered Algy, and fastened his clown's hat on with elastic. He was very embarrassed, snorted and licked my hands and pretended to have a sneezing fit as he tried to remove the hat and frill without hurting my feelings. Then I called Ajax, and no one can tell me that dogs do not laugh! If they do not, then what was it that Algy did when he looked at Ajax? Ajax stood like an imposing statue suffering a New Year's celebration indignity as I put his cap and frill on, and Algy's face simply split in half! Algy finally wore his decorations meekly, but Ajax tore his hat and frill off and chewed them to pulp.

We got the audience seated, Mrs Carter had to be pushed up the ladder fore and aft but finally she made it; and then we began our programme. I stood in the middle of the ring with a long stock-whip in my hand, while Garth, dressed as an Indian, cantered around standing up on Buck's fat little rump. Then Benny and Kiko rode Buck all by themselves – though between the large bows on Benny's neck and on Kiko's too the little monkey was practically hidden.

After that we took turns riding the calves we had tethered outside, sitting facing their tails in the approved bush style, and getting well thrown for our pains. Then Matilda hopped in, and she and Garth wrestled, which they both always enjoyed. Matilda caught the boy in a firm grip and seemed to be trying to peer into his eye before she suddenly let him go, poked him in the tummy with her long toe, and then hopped gracefully away! Garth laughed so much he had to sit down to get over it, and the audience clapped loudly.

After that there were several more 'acts', and I put on my Eastern costume for my snake-charming act. I ran to the stump to get Kaa, and he was not there. I searched for him, but there were no signs of him anywhere, so I went into the ring and did what I hoped was an Indian dance to the music of the gramophone which we had installed in the shed.

My act was the last one, and after the applause I went into the lower room, where the party was all laid out on the trestle table, with the chairs set primly around, and the large wicker chair standing imposingly at the end of the table waiting for the guest of honour to take it.

My father's feet appeared on the top rungs of the ladder, then Mrs Carter's prim black shoes, as he steadied her to the accompaniment of her little squeals. In a moment they would be right in the room, and then my eye caught sight of something queer about the wicker chair – I could not believe it. I looked again – and it was true. There, curled round the seat, was Kaa, a sure passport to hysteria for Mrs Carter! I knew that she would think we had arranged this, Garth would be so upset, and our parents very angry indeed.

Kaa was sleeping blissfully, and in an instant it would be too late to do anything, for he was so heavy I could never get him out before he was seen and the whole party became a dismal failure. I could only think of one thing to do: I snatched off my Indian shawl, spread it over Kaa, and lowered myself gently on to his coils. He barely moved, he was used to my sitting on him, and obligingly shifted a little so that I could sit comfortably. I clung to the arms of the chair, terrified that he would decide to come out from under the shawl and spoil everything. I kept very still, and sat looking very red-faced and nervous.

Mrs Carter and my father stepped down into the room, while the rest of the party climbed down. My father turned to face me and called:

'Hullo! What are you doing at the head of the table – come on, get off the best chair, you little monkey!'

I was speechless, and Garth came in.

'Hey!' he said, 'I carried that chair up here for Mrs Carter, not for you!'

Mrs Carter walked towards me, and I was so terrified I burst out:

'Oh, Mrs Carter, do *please* let me sit here – I – do really want to so much!'

My father began to say 'Nonsense!' and Garth came towards me as if he was going to pull me off the chair, when the old lady saved her own bacon, and sat down graciously at the other end of the table, saying:

'Of course, dear – no, please don't move her, why, the child was the star of the show, so she should have the star's seat!'

I felt awful. Garth was glaring at me furiously, everyone else looked very disapproving, and they determined to ignore me completely. I was so miserable, and then Kaa began to move and heaved me up and down. Nessie said sharply:

'Little girls should sit still at table!'

And how I wished I could! Garth sat alternately glaring at me and beaming at the thick icing on his cake; then during one glare I saw his expression change, and I felt a soft 'tap tap' up my back, as Kaa uncoiled his head and neck and began mildly feeling his way up my spine. I sat quite still, wondering what the result would be if his flat head and lidless eyes suddenly peered over my shoulder. But by now I had an ally; my brother understood, and it was his turn to look horrified. He hurriedly shoved the cake into his mouth, and to my relief I felt Kaa's head slide down. The restless coils settled and I knew he would keep quiet for a little while longer, even though I had been heaving up and down while everyone glared at me and said 'Keep still'.

It was a great relief when tea was over and the grown-ups began moving towards the car. I still sat as if I were nailed to the seat of the throne of honour. My parents looked rather surprised, but decided that if I was determined to behave so badly they would simply ignore me. Finally the last one filed out, leaving Nessie, Lewis and Garth with me. I began to sob miserably, but I soon perked up when I showed the sleeping Kaa, and was told that I had done exactly the right thing, and that my mother and father would be very proud of me when they knew.

15. Luck Takes a Hand

With my brother's return to school, the old worry about being sent off to boarding school myself after the mid-winter holidays, which meant about the end of July, began to crowd in on me once again. The thought of leaving my home, my dogs, all the people I loved, was so dreadful to me that I could not speak about it even to my mother. I think both she and Brownie understood this, but my father insisted that for my own sake I must go where I could be among other children, and neither of them knew how to comfort me. I spent every minute of the day when I could be alone in slipping away with the dogs, going again and again to all our favourite haunts, and a great deal of the nights lying awake in my verandah bed, while the sounds I loved came through the velvety night air, the call of a possum, the wail of a dingo, or the steady, surging sound of yarded cattle, all a part of my short life and almost as dear to me as Algy's loud snorings – which never disturbed me in the least. I would lie with my hand over the edge of the bed touching Ajax's great head, feeling Benny's warm little body on my feet, and with my heart full of desolation and foreboding.

The dogs and I once did some fishing – not fishing as you know it, but a rather more dangerous game. In our game, fishing waters were replaced by an old, dried-up well; the fishing line and the bait were a silk handkerchief, and the fish were the deadly Australian black snakes.

These snakes grow to about seven or eight feet long. They are very poisonous, but like most wild creatures, they are only dangerous if you frighten them. I always worried a lot that the dogs might attack one, but as they were used to Kaa, and I had tried to teach them to leave other snakes alone, they were fairly safe. Once I saw Algy sniffing about a patch of grass, and a black snake reared itself up out of it with its tongue flickering almost on Algy's snub nose; I was afraid to call out in case he might turn to me and the snake would strike, so I stayed quite still, and the snake doubled back on itself and disappeared – perhaps it could not bear to bite that silly, friendly, darling dog!

It was Lewis who showed me how to fish for snakes in the old well. The well was about fifteen feet deep with only about an inch of water at the bottom. The sides were faced with old planks, and tufts of grass grew where the boards had rotted away. The sides were dotted here and there with small round holes. We kept very quiet, and presently a flat head, with dull eyes and flickering tongue, poked out of one of the holes. When the head was well out Lewis lowered a silk handkerchief corner-wise to the snake. As the tip touched it the snake dodged back into its hole, but when it put its head out Lewis bobbed the handkerchief up and down and in a flash the snake struck. Lewis jerked the hanky, the snake ducked its head back, and one of its poison fangs came up in the end of the hanky.

My fishing was not so successful, but I had a lot of fun trying. Of course I knew that I should not fish without Lewis, but one day I did. Peering into the well I saw two heads, and this was too much for me. I ran home and got one of my father's big silk handkerchiefs – Brownie always polished my hair with it – tied a piece of string to the corner, and began fishing.

I missed three catches, and became very absorbed in

Lewis showed me how to fish for snakes.

what I was doing. Then I heard a yelp and a sliding, scratching sound, lumps of soil fell into the well, and the head I was fishing for disappeared. I looked up; to my horror Ben was half-way down the well, digging his claws in, but sliding very quickly towards the bottom in a shower of rubble.

Algy began whining and scratching at the rim, and Ben, on the bottom by now and quite unhurt, barked furiously for help, and danced about on his short hind legs that always seemed to have furry plus-fours covering his tiny hams. He peered upwards, and scolded me for all he was worth.

I was very worried. I did not know how to get Ben up, nor did I know how many snakes were down that well, nor how long they would stand the rumpus Ben was making. I dragged Algy to a stump and tied him up with my belt, and had to scold him to make him stay there; poor old fellow, he was very bewildered, he knew he was only trying to help Ben. Then Ajax and I raced for Lewis, who was busy carpentering. He went into his toolshed and brought out a piece of supple greased rope and we hurried back to the well.

We found Benny simply hoarse with rage at being deserted.

Lewis set to work to lassoo him, but he was no help at all in his own rescue dancing and wriggling and trying to avoid the lassoo, while all the time I held my breath and watched for a deadly head and lissom body to appear from one of the holes. Finally Lewis did get the noose round the ungrateful little dog, and he was hauled up, gasping for breath as the rope tightened round his chest: once up, he scolded and growled at everybody, and was not at all grateful for being saved.

After that the well was boarded up, and the dogs and I had to go back to river fishing. The river was very low, and in patches it was so thick with river weed that I had to use the oar like a punt-pole to get through. Algy, who hated water, evidently thought the weed was grass, because one day I heard a great splash behind me, and Algy came to the surface draped in weeds like some river monster, gasping and very frightened, and I managed to haul him into the boat, shipping gallons of weedy water at the same time. Poor Algy, he never made the same mistake again.

One of our odd-job men was an Aborigine, who called himself 'King Billy'. He used to chop wood – when he could not help himself, and he wore a strange costume, his everyday rags topped by an old black silk top hat given to him by my English grandfather. Billy loved it, and when he wore it he changed his title from 'King' to 'General', as a compliment to my grandfather and his regiment!

Billy was an expert fisherman in the Abo style, with long spears instead of hooks and lines. He would push the boat into shallow water, stand in the prow, spot a fish and throw the spear with beautiful accuracy. This way the fish is pinned to the bed of the river, and the quivering shaft is there to mark the spot. My fishing in this way was not very good, but I enjoyed trying, and I *was* rather handicapped: Ajax kept quiet in the boat, but those sterling hunters Ben and Algy rushed from side to side, which made it difficult to balance a spear and myself. When Billy was fishing I kept the dogs quiet, but they fussed so when Billy tried to hold them that I found it easier to accept the handicap. One day, when I saw a big fish swimming lazily by, I launched the spear – and myself as well! I came an awful flop and Ajax jumped in after me, while the other two rushed to the side of the boat and nearly turned it over. In the end I clambered in, in spite of the loving kisses from Algy and Ben and the fuss they made over me, which kept pushing me back into the water again.

Those strange Australian creatures, the platypuses, funny little throw-backs to another age, were very plentiful every now and again in our river. The platypus is shy and is protected by law, but the high price of its fur makes poaching go on. From earlier days my parents had a rug of platyus skins; it was a short fur, brownish grey and very hard-wearing, rather like beaver.

Sometimes, lazing about on the quiet reaches of the river, I have seen half a dozen platypuses floating quietly on the surface, oblongs of brown fur. At the slightest movement, they would flip their bodies beneath the water in a flash. They are about a foot long, with duck bills and webbed feet with spurs on the back ones – these are said to be poisonous. They build their nests in a sort of tunnel dug right up through the roots of the large trees edging the banks. Their babies are born in winter, usually two at a time, and are like smooth, fat, whitish grubs.

The time to find the nests is when a white frost is on the ground, early on a winter's morning. Then Lewis would take me along the bank, the grass-blades, little javelins of ice, sticking through my sandals, until we saw a small circle of grass without frost, always near the trunk of a tree. Then Lewis began a careful digging, and the dogs had to be restrained from helping, because to disturb a platypus nest roughly may make the mother desert the babies.

We scooped the last of the earth away with our hands very gently, and there, on a nest of soil and sticks, lay two tiny babies, fat and helpless. When we had seen them we would replace the sticks, leaves and earth very carefully indeed. Platypuses have become more and more scarce, for they are gentle, defenceless creatures, and their only weapon is their speed.

Life was lazily full of the things I loved, and I would

have been well content but for the lurking misery that hung over everything when I remembered suddenly that in a few months I would be far away from all this. Then one mail-day, which only happened twice a week, I came walking home at sunset, and saw my mother in the distance coming towards me. We met and she turned to walk back with me, and told me that my father had had a letter from the school – it had been impossible to find a vacancy for me until the new year. I was saved, at least temporarily, and that night I slept soundly without long wakeful hours of misery and weeping.

16. A Desperate Adventure

Australia is such a land of extremes that it is difficult to know whether floods or droughts are the worst, but I think that living through a really bad drought is about as nasty a thing as you can imagine. People living on stations depend upon the rivers for everything except drinking water, which is caught from the rain on iron roofs, and drained off into tanks. In a long drought fruit trees and vegetables die, and of course there are no flowers. What little water there is in the tanks has to be kept only for drinking, and even washing-up water, and water used for tea or cooking, has to be boiled river-water, hauled daily and kept in big barrels. The river itself becomes horrible, just a chain of stagnant pools, more like a weed-choked lake than a river, all green and slimy and full of dead river creatures.

Animals suffer badly, droves of stock die of thirst and starvation, and the barren earth is dotted with bodies, so that a dreadful smell of death lies over the land. Although there are frequent short droughts, the long droughts only happen now and again. Then there is great danger of fire, for every blade of grass, every tree and piece of fallen timber becomes tinder ready to blaze at the slightest spark; perhaps from lightning, or from the sun shining on a piece of broken glass, or from ash dropped by a careless smoker.

I remember a drought like this when the brazen heat of the sun poured down week after week, month after month, and the air was thick and smoke-filled from far-off fires. Even poor old Algy, who hated water, would throw himself panting into the still, weedy edge of the river for coolness, and rise again looking like a bunyip, the Aborigines' fabulous river monster.

The biggest drought I remember began around Inverell, which was about seventy miles from Gunyan. When the annual show-time came round, the townspeople decided to go on with it in spite of the bad season, and although it was very poorly attended there were the usual merry-go-rounds, sideshows, and a big circus. Then a tragedy happened; the circus was almost destroyed by fire. Some of the animals were burnt in their cages, and others escaped, all of which were recaptured, except three wolves which disappeared into the wild country round about. Hunts were organized, and occasionally farmers reported raided fowl houses; one man said he saw three gaunt grey forms leap over his hen-house fence, and that he fired at the last one and thought, from the trail of blood it left, that he must have shot it in the hind leg. The poor brutes must have been very hungry, for there is not much to eat about a droughty land, and when nothing was heard of them for some weeks people thought they must have moved up north where there was more food and less vigilance.

As the drought spread round my home, my father was busy hiring drovers to move the stock on agisted land, where the owners got so much a head for the grazing rights when they had the luck to have more rain than their neighbours. Droughts were particularly hard on the small land owners. Gunyan was a big station with an area of about a hundred square miles, so there was usually some corner of it where a little feed could be found; but about fourteen miles above Gunyan a nice English couple who had bought a block of land were having a very bad time. My parents helped where they could, sending meat and vegetables to them as long as we had any.

Then Mrs Graham, the wife of this new squatter, sent my mother a note to say that she had been unexpectedly landed with her sister's children, two little girls, one about my own age and one younger, while their mother went into hospital for a few weeks. She begged my mother to let me stay with them for the week-end; the children were homesick and miserable and she thought it would make a great difference to them to have another child to play with. But – would I please leave the dogs at home, as there was always trouble between them and Mr Graham's thoroughbred cattle dogs, and right now they simply could not have the dogs put out of action in the struggle to move the drought-stricken stock.

Of course I did not want to go. I hated the thought of leaving the dogs, and I was rather scared of the children; also, the wonderful reprieve I had had from boarding school in July was running out, and only another two months remained before I was to be sent as a boarder to the Armidale girls' school. Back had came all the worrying and fretting, the long tearful nights, filled with dreadful anticipations of homesickness and longing for my dogs.

However, under the circumstances my mother thought that I should go to the Grahams, and very reluctantly I agreed. It was arranged for me to ride over on the Friday afternoon and back on Sunday. Mr Graham said he would ride halfway to meet me, which I privately thought was rather silly, as I was used to riding alone much greater distances than the fourteen miles between Gunyan and Baroona.

I was very miserable about Ajax, Ben and Algy – it seemed to me that I had so little time left with them that it was dreadful to have to give up two whole days of it. My going away meant that they would have to be shut up in a big, airy stable at night, so that they could not follow me, and in the day-time my mother promised to keep them about the house with her. But anyway I hated the thought. Benny would be all right, he was so vain and self-important that he would rather enjoy howling for me, and being comforted by my mother, and allowed all sorts of little privileges he did not get when I was home. I pictured Algy's lined bull-dog face with its flat nose pressed against the wire netting that covered the verandah, sitting patiently hour after hour, waiting for my return. But Ajax, my splendid half dingo of a dog, would be filled with the savage despair that always took possession of him when he was out of my sight, and there was nothing anyone could do that would comfort him, and I felt he was paying far too great a price for the pleasure of two silly little stranger-girls.

Still, I was made to go, and there was just nothing I could do about it. So I said a sad good-bye to my boys as I shut them into the stable with plenty of out-sized bones, their own blankets, my blue woollen dressing-gown, which they all loved and always managed to pull off my bed, and a promise from Brownie and my mother to make all the fuss they could of them.

As I had outgrown Buck I rode my beautiful chestnut mare, Belle, who was as lively as Buck was sluggish and considerably more fun to ride. I rode off miserably enough, thinking about the dogs, followed by Benny's and Algy's yaps and howls, and Ajax's deep cry, as long as I was within earshot. The earth was bare and barren along the way, and it was very hot. Mr Graham met me, and by the time we reached the house and I had been introduced to Kathleen and Enid, and had a sumptuous piece of thickly-iced chocolate cake, I felt just a little better.

If I had not been so worried about the dogs it would have been a very happy week-end, because after the first shyness had worn off the little girls and I got on splendidly, and Mrs Graham said they might come to Gunyan for the next week-end. I smiled when I thought how cross Buck would be when he found out what was in store for him! Mrs Graham was very nice about the dogs, and told me she was so sorry she had to ask me to leave them behind; but I did see why, Algy and Ajax were so large, and they were often very naughty about fighting.

We woke on Sunday morning to find the air searingly hot, and black rolling clouds of smoke on the horizon. The dry, scorching wind brought charred particles of wood and dead insects into the house. That dread thing, a bush-fire, had started in an upper paddock. Mr Graham got his few men together, and they left to fight it. He said he would be back by five o'clock, so as to ride part-way home with me, which would give me time to get back before it was dark, about eight. Mrs Graham wanted me to wait until Monday, but as there was no telephone between Baroona and Gunyan I knew my parents would worry, besides, I did not want to leave the dogs any longer. So in the end she agreed I could go, especially as none of the men could be spared to take a message, and when my father knew about the fire he would be sure to send some help, which was badly needed.

It was after five that we saw a horseman coming slowly towards us. He was a son of one of the stockmen, a boy of about sixteen, utterly exhausted his eyes blood-red from the smoke, and his hair and eyebrows singed by the flames he had been fighting. Mrs Graham gave him a cool drink and made him sit down. Then he told us that Mr Graham simply could not leave the fire, and he must keep every hand with him. He had sent George back to get the spring cart and to bring back drinking water and food in it, as they must stay there all night.

The fire had gained so much way that when night fell the sky glowed with it, and my parents would be very anxious if I had not reached home. Mr Graham needed help more than ever, and Mrs Graham, worried to distraction as she was, finally agreed that it was rather silly to insist on anyone going half-way with me when I was used to riding anywhere I chose by myself and I knew every inch of the way – including a short cut, which I had not taken on my way over for fear of missing Mr Graham.

It was nearly six o'clock by the time I rode away, leaving Mrs Graham bustling about the kitchen, helped by the girls, getting the food and drink ready for the fire-fighters. I rode off at a brisk canter, hurrying to get home before my parents began to worry about me. A couple of miles from Baroona I decided to turn off the rough bush track I was following, and to take the short cut I knew about. Then a few miles from the turn-off I found that a new wire fence had been put up since I had been that way months before. It was a nuisance, as the short cut would only have saved a couple of miles, and the wire fence would delay me longer than it would take to ride that far. Still, there was nothing for it, I could not get through or over the wire. There was a post and rail fence a mile or two away from the direction I was going in, however, and I decided it would be shorter to follow the wire fence up to this, because I was sure I could pull a top rail off somewhere, and then jump Belle over the lower one, and this way I would soon make up the extra distance.

When I did reach the rail fence I had an awful job pulling out a rail, I simply was not strong enough, but finally I managed it, and got Belle over the lower rail.

Then I had to replace the heavy top one in case some of the stock got through, and this took a long time too. When I finished this it was beginning to get dark, with that swift completeness that is typical of Australia, when you are left feeling like a bird in a cage over which a dark cover has been flung.

I hurried Belle along and we cantered over the brown, shrivelled ground. I could not see where I was riding, but I knew that Belle would take me in the general direction of home. Once I heard the blood-curdling, mournful howl of a dingo from the dry bed of a small gulley on my left, and on top of the bank I thought that for a moment I saw the animal's glowing eyes. I urged Belle on. I was not frightened of dingoes; deadly as they are to stock, I had never heard of their attacking humans, and they never hunt in packs. A whole family of dingoes may stick together for a while when the pups are young, but once they grow up dingoes become lone hunters.

Belle was almost galloping when suddenly I felt her lurch forward. She hit the ground and I must have sailed over her head and knocked myself out, for all I remember is a sharp pain in my shoulder, then complete darkness. After goodness knows how long, I began a slow coming-to from some cold, black, far away place of the senses.

I tried to sit up, but the sharp pain in my left shoulder made me stop. My left ankle hurt dreadfully, and my head throbbed, so that I seemed to be seeing everything in a blur, for the bright starlight made it possible to see the blurred outlines of a few tree stumps that were around me.

Again I heard that mournful, wavering howl from somewhere in the darkness, and my throbbing scalp prickled with a fear I did not understand. I realized that I must try and do something, but I did not know exactly what. There was no sign of Belle, but I could only see a few yards into the darkness, and anyway by the dreadful pain in my shoulder I guessed something must have broken, and I would never be able to mount the mare. I hoped that she was all right and that she would make for home, because then a search party would come for me and Ajax would find me very quickly. I knew that the mare must have stepped into a rabbit hole, and come down herself, and probably thrown me some distance, and I only prayed that she had not broken a leg, and was not lying somewhere just out of my sight, suffering miserably.

Suddenly a pair of eyes shone greenly in the darkness a few yards away, then another pair appeared beside the first – and another! I was afraid. I felt a small stick under my hand and tried to throw it. The movement hurt dreadfully, but the three pairs of eyes disappeared, only to reappear a few yards farther to my right. It was painful to turn my head, but I did, and saw a twisted tree a few yards behind me; setting my teeth, I dragged myself along the ground towards it. I knew I could not climb into it, but at least it was something solid at my back, and I felt a slowly growing fear of those burning green eyes.

I could only move a few inches at a time, and my face was wet with pain and exertion. Then I must have fainted because I came to with a horrible animal smell in my nostrils. I opened my eyes and stared straight into a pair of glaring eyes above a long dark muzzle. I yelled, and the gaunt form leaped backwards: then I saw that it was not a dingo, it was much taller and rangier than any full-blooded dingo could be, and it had not the dingo's characteristic golden coat that turns to a pale silver by starlight. This creature had been a shaggy dark grey – and suddenly I knew that those three pairs of eyes belonged to the wolves that had escaped from the circus.

My heart leaped with terror. The small movements I made kept them back for the moment, but they would not do so for long, and I had no way to defend myself. I doubted that I could even get as far as the tree, and anyway it would not help. The wolves were hungry, they had been ranging a drought-stricken country where game had vanished – so what chance did a badly injured girl have against three of them maddened with hunger?

I wanted to cry, but somehow that seemed such a useless thing to do that I kept my tears back. As usual when I was in trouble I thought of Ajax. I had always known that between my dog and me there was some strange instinct that told us when the other one was in trouble. Whatever it was, I believed that something would tell Ajax that I was in great need of him, and that he would come to me, and I raised my voice and called as loudly as I could:

'Ajax! Ajax! Come to me, I need you!'

Now that my eyes were used to the darkness, and the fierce, stabbing pains in my head were a little better, I could see the three lean, hungry forms moving round me in circles, round and round, frightening shadows that circled monotonously, always closing in a little. Their eyes gleamed as they turned their heads in the starlight, going round and round and round, in the way the Red Indians circled encampments of covered wagons in the Frontier days.

I began to feel light-headed; it was a nightmare watching those silent forms circling, circling. I noticed that the one bringing up the rear did not lope silently like the other two, for he limped badly and made a small, dry, rustling sound as his lame foot dragged a little on the parched ground.

Suddenly they stopped circling and threw their heads up, and the hungry, mournful cry I heard earlier came from their shaggy throats. Again my scalp prickled, but I had passed the apex of my terror, and now in all the pain and confusion I seemed to be standing outside my body and watching those poor, famished beasts in a way that seemed to be unconnected with my own danger. Their wails died away, and they began their endless circling again – then one broke from the circle and rushed towards me. I did not make a conscious movement; without my will my right foot kicked out and the wolf leapt back. The pain of the movement was terrible, and I thought that I was fainting again, and tried desperately not to, staring hard at the three forms, and as the faintness passed away I noticed that the circling had stopped and all three beasts were standing with their backs to me, listening intently to something I could not hear.

And then I did hear something, a sound that meant life itself to me, the thud of great feet on the dry earth – and Ajax leapt out of the darkness to my side, and put his golden muzzle for an instant against my face before he whirled to face my three enemies.

The wolves had turned too, and stood facing us, the leader slightly in advance, and one wolf on each side of him. Now my fears for myself turned to a sickening, desperate fear for Ajax. Those great gaunt, hunger-ridden bodies, the long cruel heads, were filled with the power and savagery of the wild. They were the most terrible enemies my dog had ever faced. Ajax was taller and heavier than the largest wolf, but there were three of them, and they were all crazed with hunger. There was nothing I could do.

Ajax breathed deeply and evenly as he always did before a fight, and the only sound he made was a sort of faint, shuddering growl deep in his chest. The wolves were quite silent, their eyes gleaming in the starlight. The leader took a stiff-legged step forward. The others followed him and I felt Ajax move forward from me. Again that small movement forward, and I knew that my Ajax was steady as a rock, and balanced to meet the swiftest rush, with all the cunning and power of his own wild ancestors pitted against the deadly, pack-fighting knowledge of the strangers. Then the leader rushed forward with incredible swiftness, his head low, his jaws aimed for Ajax's front legs to cripple him, while the other two sprang higher to bear him down with their weight. Ajax was ready for them; he leapt sideways, his quick slash ripped the leader's shoulder wide open, and the leaping blood shone dark in the starlight.

Then I found I could not follow the fight in the half-light. There was no sound except the breathing of the fighters, and the clash of teeth when a savage slash missed the flesh. I saw a great grey form go hurtling through the air and lie still, but Ajax and the leader fought on, while the lame wolf kept darting in, slashing at Ajax and leaping clumsily back again. Ajax must have decided to end these harrying tactics from the rear, for as the lame wolf retreated from one attack behind its leader Ajax gave a great leap right over the leader's head, and with a crunch of his jaws he left the lame wolf on the ground, and whirled round to take the leader's return rush.

Sometimes I closed my eyes to shut out these grim, struggling figures fighting, as it seemed to me, for an eternity, but all the time my ears were filled with the dry sound of their rushing feet, the gasps and thuds of body on body, the clash and snap of jaws, their heavy, laboured breathing ... would it never end? I began to despair.

My eyes were shut tight when suddenly the sounds of the struggle stopped and I felt heavy breathing against my face. For an instant I was in a panic and

The wolves turned and stood facing him.

could not open my eyes. Then I opened them, and saw a great, blood-stained form beside me, slashed and torn and with one leg badly mangled – Ajax. I pressed my face against his reddened muzzle, and cried bitterly as I had not been able to cry for myself, and I knew that in his own way he was telling me that all was well.

Around me I could see the big forms of the three fallen wolves, and as I stopped sobbing Ajax limped over to the leader, sniffed at him, and then raised his muzzle to the sky to give his long, wavering call of victory, a call that was akin to the hunger-cries the wolves had given earlier on. I could not struggle any more. I slumped down on to the ground and Ajax lay beside me, and it was like that my father and Lewis found us.

They told me that Ajax had become very restless about dusk, and that as soon as Belle arrived home trailing her bridle they let Ajax out of the stable and he was off in a flash on Belle's trail, far ahead of them before they could get the horses saddled, collect torches, and make a slower progress. Belle's tracks were not easy to follow on the hard, dry earth, and with no light but the torches.

They heard Ajax's victorious cry and found us a few minutes afterwards, stumbling first over the body of one wolf before they saw the other two, and then Ajax, close beside me.

Now that the excitement was over, the pain was really bad, and the men picked me up and put a pad under my left arm to ease the pain from my broken collarbone. They could do nothing about my badly-twisted ankle, or what proved to be slight concussion, which began to affect my eyesight. Lewis tore up his handkerchief and bandaged Ajax's badly bitten leg; the other wounds had to wait. Then, carrying me very gently, and with Ajax following on three legs, they turned towards home, leading the horses until they got to where it was possible to bring the car to take us the rest of the way.

There Ajax and I waited with my father, while Lewis rode quickly home, prepared my mother for the sight of me, and drove the car back. My mother telephoned for the doctor. I was washed and put in my bed, and Ajax, his wounds cleaned and his leg properly attended to, lay beside me on the verandah.

My mother insisted that I should be kept very quiet, but I could hear my father and Lewis talking in the room next to me. Lewis said:

'So that's what happened to the three wolves from the circus; queer their coming down into the droughty country –'

'I suppose the number of people hunting for them up North made it even harder for them to get food.'

'Yes. I'll get the skins tomorrow – you may as well have something out of this; let Ajax lie on a rug made of his enemies.'

'Ajax – there isn't anything in the world that Ajax wants and I can give him that he can't have.'

I knew that Lewis was smiling as he said:

'The nice thing about Ajax is that he *has* what he wants, and he is prepared to die to keep it!'

After a time the doctor came and the next hour was pretty bad for me, the setting of the collar bone and the touching of my ankle hurt a great deal, and the pain made me wide awake instead of sleepy. I could not make a fuss, because if I had Ajax would have stopped the doctor from touching me. As it was he did not like it very much, but it took my mind off myself to try and keep him from worrying – and he had certainly earned it.

When the doctor finished my mother stayed on with me, and the doctor went in to talk to my father. Their voices came clearly out on to the verandah, and I heard something that seemed to make it all worth while. I heard the doctor say firmly to my father:

'The child's tough enough. Physically she'll be all right as soon as that collar-bone sets, but she has had a terrible shock and it may take her years to get over it. Of course you must give up the idea of sending her away to school, probably for years. Keep her at home where she's happy, never mind about anything else; she's been fretting about boarding school, I know, and it must stop, she must not have anything to worry her until she is quite over this.'

I looked at my mother and she smiled down at me. Indeed it had been worth it, and I felt that Ajax would think so too.

I put my hand over the edge of the bed and touched the gaunt, silken head of my dog Ajax, slashed and marred in my defence; on my other side Algy snored loudly, and in the crook of my sound arm little Ben, the mighty hunter, yipped in his dreams. I went to sleep with the sound, the sight, the security of my world all around me – undisturbed and beautiful.

PRACTIC
AND RENC
COLO

ALSO BY THE SAME AUTHOR

No BP31 PRACTICAL ELECTRICAL RE-WIRING AND REPAIRS

PRACTICAL REPAIR AND RENOVATION OF COLOUR TVs

by

CHAS. E. MILLER

BABANI PRESS
The Publishing Division of
Babani Trading and Finance Co. Ltd.
The Grampians
Shepherds Bush Road
London W6 7NF
England.

I.S.B.N. 0 85934 037 6

First Published – December 1976
Reprinted – December 1979

Printed and Manufactured in Great Britain by
C. Nicholls & Co. Ltd.

CONTENTS

FOREWORD

There is little doubt that many enthusiasts would love to be able to build their own colour television receivers, and to experience the thrill and satisfaction that this enterprise would bring. Unfortunately, if we are honest, it has to be admitted that it is just not a practical proposition. The few designs which have appeared in the last few years have relied to a large extent upon commercially produced circuit boards, which must be fitted with components and soldered at home. This is of necessity an expensive and time-consuming job, with the ever present risk of making a mistake which could take an awful long time to be discovered. It is immeasurably more difficult to find a fault on a previously untried piece of equipment than it is with the commercial equivalent which must have been working when it left the factory! It is not surprising, therefore, that there has no boom in home-constructed colour sets, as there was with black-and-white back in the 50s. At that time many different component firms offered kits of parts to constructors; the fact that this has not happened in the eight years or so since colour TV was established is significant.

Recently, however, a state of affairs has arisen which is of considerable interest to enthusiasts. The ever rising costs of repairs to the older colour TVs has resulted in large numbers becoming available on the second-hand market. The price of a set in working condition can be anything from £50-£150, but non-workers may be obtained for as little as tens of pounds. Very often such sets have been written off by dealers as "B.E.R." – Beyond Economical Repair. This is fully understandable when one takes into account the cost of a technician's time alone, without the price of spare parts. A day's work on a set could easily result in a bill to the customer (who can be the dealer himself if it is a rented-out set) of £30 or more, plus VAT, which at present adds another 12½%. But for the enthusiast it is a very different story. He does not have to think that "time is money". Indeed, he will thoroughly enjoy the hours of spare time he will spend on renovating a potentially useful set.

The object of this book is to assist firstly in the choice and acquisition of a second-hand colour TV; and secondly to deal step by step with common faults and their cures in order to get it in good order. If you are inclined to doubt your ability, take heart. Colour TV has been around in the United States for many years. A well-known American service engineer, Jack Darr, wrote long ago that in his experience a very large proportion of colour TV faults were attributable to the same causes as with monochrome sets; namely failed resistors, capacitors, and valves. This statement is still valid today, except that semi-conductors must now be added to the list.

As to equipment, although it would be nice to have transistor testers, oscilloscopes, pattern generators and so on to hand, it is by no means essential. A good multi-meter will serve to trace all but the most obscure faults. The transmitted testcard will enable convergence to be adjusted to an acceptable standard. Provided that you can adopt a logical approach to problems you should be quite capable of solving them. And once you have gained a little experience, confidence will follow.

What this book is not intended to be is a detailed guide to the PAL colour system. This would require a volume in itself. Obviously the basic functions must be understood if renovation is undertaken, and a general outline is given in Chapter Two. Later on in the book the decoder is discussed in more depth, as this part of the set is by far the most complex. Nevertheless, most of the faults you are likely to encounter will yield to systematic use of the test meter.

There is an enormous satisfaction to be had in restoring a colour TV to active life, and to see pictures appear on the screen. It has certainly not palled for the author, after many years of doing it professionally!

CHAPTER ONE

Obtaining a Second-hand Colour TV

From the enthusiast's point of view, the sets which will be of most interest as regards availability and price are those dual standard models produced between around 1967 and 1970. It will be recalled that colour, and indeed UHF in general, was restricted to BBC2 until the autumn of 1969, thus making it necessary for the early model sets to be also capable of receiving BBC1 and ITV on 405 lines, VHF. It is this first generation of colour TVs that is now coming onto the market at as low as tens of pounds.

Where do they come from? One suggestion, made in the foreword, is that some sets are "beyond economic repair", and are consigned to store-rooms. They are likely to be joined by others taken in part-exchange against new sets. It is not really a commercial proposition for dealers to renovate and sell these sets because of the need to guarantee them for a reasonable time in accordance with consumer protection laws. It is far better for sets to be disposed of once and for all, even though the prices have to be lowered drastically. In a lot of cases this means entering them at small local auction sales, and it is always worth having a look around these in search of bargains. (But do take care; whilst preparing this chapter the author examined a modern-looking colour TV offered for sale under the hammer, only to find that the tube had been replaced with a monochrome type!) Any sets not actually described as in working order seldom make much money in auctions. Depending upon the age and condition, a maximum of around £35 is reasonable. Sets which have scruffy cabinets can be had for much less than this. It may be worth your while enquiring at local dealers to see if they will sell an old set to you directly. You must, of course make it clear that you are prepared to accept it "as seen", and will not expect any kind of guarantee. Purchasing in this manner will probably cost you more than from an auction, but on the credit side the dealer or one of his engineers will most likely be able to outline what work is needed to get the set into working order.

A hign proportion of sets are rented out, and as the rental firms' profits are directly related to the reliability of their sets, it makes sense for them to sell off the older ones before they start to give trouble. Because of the large quantities involved they normally go to trade disposal concerns who in turn pass them on to the second-hand dealers and sometimes directly to the public. If there is such a firm operating near you it will pay to make enquiries. Very often they too will be only too pleased to find a customer for non-working sets.

From time to time you will find second-hand sets offered in the small-ad columns of your local papers. It may be worth your while following these up, with the following reservations. The price should be attractive, even when dealing with sets allegedly in working order, since it would be difficult to get any legal redress if serious faults were later discovered. Try to discover in a discreet manner, the reason for the sale. Genuine people are unlikely to resent your asking. And above all, don't buy what appears to be a recent model at a bargain price without seeing proof of ownership on the vendor's part. This request again will only upset those with something to hide; better that than finding yourself in possession of a set which is the property of an H.P. company!

What to look for in non-working sets

In the absence of any reliable information as to age and condition, a systematic series of checks should be carried out. Quite candidly, the actual age of the set is not likely to be too important, except as a bargaining point when fixing a price. It can often be ascertained merely by having a good look around the inside of the cabinet with a torch, as makers frequently stamp the date of manufacture on the woodwork. Alternatively the larger electrolytic capacitors are usually dated; although there will have been a time lag between their manufacture and subsequent use, it will give a good enough idea for our purpose.

Again, the outward appearance of the set will have a bearing on the price asked, and it is reasonable to expect that a set having an unmarked cabinet will have spent little time being taken in and out of the workshop. Check if all the back screws are fitted, and if they are all of the same type. Discrepancies here point to frequent servicing. It's always a good omen when the ventilation holes in the back are bunged up with dust, and the "works" also liberally coated, indicating no recent need of repairs.

If you are able to test the c.r.t. with an instrument like that to be described later in this book, you will know its conditions swiftly and accurately. When this is not possible, play safe and assume that you may have to fit a replacement when haggling.

The next most expensive item in the set is the line output transformer. This is normally enclosed in a metal shield (in the case of those using valve EHT rectifiers and stabilisers this prevents harmful X-radiation, and must be in place). If the shielding is wholly- or partly-missing, or appears to have been recently disturbed, trouble in the LOPT may have been suspected and/or investigated. Mentally deduct about £10 from the price to cover this eventuality.

In the case of sets having separate panels for the various stages, make sure that all are present. This may sound rather obvious, but even an old hand can be fooled when glancing around an unfamiliar set.

Note if any valves are missing. Even if you are certain of obtaining cheap replacements, think in terms of the full price for bargaining purposes.

Working Sets

We will, of course, assume that the set demonstrated to you does not exhibit perfect sound and picture, which would make further comment superfluous! But it is all too easy to be convinced that a picture is "perfect" when in the grip of enthusiasm. It is far better to check a set on a test card rather than on a moving picture, as any serious faults show up immediately. Severe misconvergence will make the vertical lines look like medal ribbons, for instance. The little girl pictured in the centre circle should have a natural complexion; the teddy-bear should be green, and the upper background blue. Incorrect colours suggest that there are faults on the decoder section. An overall bias to one colour may merely be the result of bad "grey scale" adjustment, or it could be due to the failure of one or more of the guns in the c.r.t.

The noughts and crosses on the black-board are in the centre of the screen, and will show up incorrect static convergence and poor focus. This latter condition can be due to something more than just a wrong setting of the control. In sets using an EHT tripler this itself could be at fault. Or it could be that the c.r.t. is weak. As in black-and-white sets, turning up the brightness control will cause a weak tube to give a fuzzy picture. In some cases the colours will alter radically, too.

The tube tester will soon confirm or eliminate any doubts about the c.r.t., but boosting should not be attempted until after the set has been purchased, for obvious reasons!

Lack of picture height is not likely to cause serious problems, nor is a slight lack of width. Only when the picture is very narrow, with perhaps some bright vertical lines, need you suspect the line output transformer.

Faults on the sound are seldom very serious, and any shortcomings in this respect need cause no worries.

Prices:

The following are roughly appropriate to the classes of set described, when the cabinet is in good condition. Badly marked cabinets should attract £5-10 less.

Non-workers, nothing known, c.r.t. not tested: £20-25.
Same, but c.r.t. reasonable: £25-30.
Same, but c.r.t. poor: £15-20.
Workers, c.r.t. reasonable, but other faults: £35-40.
Same, but c.r.t. poor: £25-30.

These should be taken as a guide only. Obviously there will be ocassions when prices can be raised or lowered. Don't be misled into snapping up the first set you see if you have doubts about it. Second-hand colour TV is now a buyer's market, and you can afford to be a little selective.

A Survey of the Sets most readily Available

Dual-standard sets were produced under around two dozen brand names, but the number of manufacturers was only eight. This makes it relatively easy to briefly discuss the various types and to evaluate their appeal to the enthusiast. In more general terms, the majority of sets were "hybrids", i.e., they employed a mixture of valves and transistors. This usually meant that the lightly-loaded parts of the set (tuners, IF panels, decoders) employed transistors, with valves doing the hard work, especially in the line time base. This is an arrangement ideally suited to the enthusiast. Low-power transistors are cheap and freely obtainable, whilst the valves are to be had at economical prices from "surplus" dealers. This is not always so with the high-power transistors which would otherwise be used; a PL509 line output valve can cost as little as 30p, with the equivalent transistor at around £2-3. The valve, obviously, is much easier to install, whilst it usually gives some visual warning, by glowing red-hot, of trouble in the line output stage. Perhaps this accounts in part for some of the best-known makers sticking to hybrids right up to the present.

The exception was, and is the Thorn Group. Right from the start their sets were fully transistorised. This entailed the use of a very large number of semi-conductors, and considerable complication of design. For this reason, in the body of this book, Thorn chassis are dealt with separately from the hybrids, in most of the chapters.

The following descriptions are in alphabetical order of the Groups producing the relevant Brand names.

1. Baird/Radio Rentals. Most sets rented out; now filtering through to the second-hand market. Servicability good. Only snag on earlier models the use of a rotary, rather than push-button UHF tuner, but this could be modified. Spares situation could be complicated by the Thorn take-over.

2. Decca. Also produced for Granada rental concern under that name. One of the best sets for enthusiasts. Most of the works on large horizontal chassis with access from below. The Service Department is most efficient, and unfailingly helpful.

3. GEC/Masteradio/Sobell. Another well-set out chassis, with swing-up facility for tracing faults on underside of print. One snag: they are the only group to use printed panels with "wiring" on both sides. This makes changing components, etc., more difficult than with conventional types. Nevertheless, recommended, as it is generally very reliable.

4. I.T.T. (K.B. & R.G.D.) What a lot of initials! These sets are probably the least likely to be found on the second-hand market, presumably because they are so very good. Forget recent adverse reports in "Which" – these sets are extremely reliable, and well worth buying.

5. Philips Group (Alba*, Philips, Stella) Very large, heavy, and cumbersome sets. Used rather more valves than most. The upright chassis allows only limited access for servicing, and the design is what one expects of Philips-technically excellent, but very complicated in practice. Reluctantly not really recommended.

6. Pye Group (Dynatron, Ekco, Ferranti, Invicta, Pye) A good design, using easily removed sub-chassis. Highly recommended.

7. Rank (Bush, Defiant*, Murphy) The earlier hybrids were far better for servicing than the later "all-solid-state", due to the spacious layout of the former. Sub-panels not quite so easy to detach as some, but still warmly recommended.

8. Thorn (Ferguson, HMV, Marconi, Ultra) The odd man out. Fully transistorised, which gives reasonable reliability at the expense of complication, especially in the power supply unit and line timebase/ EHT oscillator. Some of the semi-conductors could be difficult/ expensive to obtain. O.K. apart from these reservations.

* Independent concern using chassis made by this manufacturer.

General

Most of these sets had large, spacious cabinets which allow good access, particularly in the case of 25" models. This also gave them plenty of ventilation space, which is probably one factor in their reliability. A tribute to this is supplied by the longevity of some of the designs; the Pye group chassis in single standard form, and with slight modifications, has been produced for many years, as an instance.

By looking around you should be able to acquire a pretty good example at a maximum of £40. Above this figure you might as well buy a good worker and miss all the fun of renovation!

P.S. Just as this book was nearing completion, a 25" Decca colour set, in a magnificent console cabinet, was sold at the author's local auction for just £7.50!

BRIEF SPECIFICATIONS OF DUAL-STANDARD COLOUR TELEVISIONS

	Tuner UHF	Units VHF	IF amps.	S.O.P.	Decoder	Lum.	C.D.A.	F.T.B.	L.T.B.	E.H.T.	Focus.
Baird	T	V	T	V	H	V	V	V	V	H	S
Decca	T	T	T	T	T	V	V	V	V	V	S
GEC	T	T	T	V	T	V	V	V	V	S	S
ITT	T	V	T	V	T	T	V	V	V	S	S
Philips	Integrated		T	V	H	V	V	V	V	V	V
Pye	Integrated		T	T	T	V	V	T	V	V	S
Rank	T	T	T	T	T	V	V	V	V	V	V
Thorn	T	T	T	T	T	T	T	T	T	S	S

V = valve   T = transistor   H = hybrid   S = solid-state

CHAPTER TWO

Basics

Before one even attempts to repair a colour TV, there are certain safety precautions which must be committed to memory so thoroughly that they become second nature. Only thus can one be sure of avoiding painful, and possibly dangerous, shocks.

Since this book is intended for enthusiasts who have "cut their teeth" on monochrome sets, it will be presumed that the reader will already be familiar with the live-chassis technique favoured by UK manufacturers. Although all colour TVs are for AC supplies only, the AC/DC type of HT supply lives on, for reasons of economy. Therefore the neutral main must be connected to the chassis of the set, normally via the black or blue conductor in the mains lead. But don't trust to luck here. Someone may have reversed the connections at the switch, or elsewhere, during maintenance work. The humble neon screwdriver will establish whether or not the chassis is live immediately, but since it is not a fail-safe device, always touch it on a known to be live part of the set (e.g., the mains fuse) to prove that it is indeed in working order.

Even with the chassis proven to be "dead" one cannot relax one's guard. All the HT points in the set will be live both to chassis and to earth- i.e., that bit of our planet that you happen to be standing upon at the time! This is why it is so much safer to work on a wooden floor, or if this is impossible, upon a wooden frame, such as a strong old door, placed on the stone or concrete.

Never work with both hands at a time, but keep one firmly in a pocket. This obviates the possibility of getting a shock from one arm to another, via the heart, which is the most dangerous kind.

Treat the EHT supply with respect. 25kV is not to be trifled with. An arc from this onto the person would almost certainly result in some nasty electrical burns, if not worse. Bear in mind, too, that the focus voltage on colour tubes is in the order of 4-5kV. The focus pin on the c.r.t. base is recognised – and avoided – by its vee-shaped insulating surround.

When the final anode connector has to be removed from a tube, always discharge the residual voltage to chassis with an insulated tool. This must be done repeatedly, as the charge builds itself up over and over again.

Reference was made in the previous chapter to valve EHT rectifiers and/or stabilisers, and to the danger of X-radiation. The makers screening around the EHT stage gives full protection, and for this reason a set must not be operated with it removed. Some firms (e.g. Philips) fitted interlock switches to positively prevent operation when the line can was dismantled. This does make life hard when searching for line time base faults, and for this reason alone sets with solid-state rectifiers are to be preferred. In a later chapter the possibility of changing from valves to solid-state will be discussed.

For fault-finding on colour sets the only absolutely essential piece of test gear is the multi-meter. It's by no means necessary to invest in transistor testers and oscilloscopes. You will already, it is presumed, have the normal range of small tools and a soldering iron or gun. The latter is excellent for heavy work (e.g., soldering direct to the chassis), but may be a little too powerful for printed panels, so it's a good plan to get hold of a fine-tipped 15 watt type as well. You will also find that an "Anglepoise" lamp is invaluable.

An item which is vitally necessary, but which may be overlooked, is a good aerial. All too often the enthusiast, relegated to a spare room or shed, relies upon a makeshift indoor type. This may have given some kind of picture on a black-and-white TV, but it just won't do for colour! You must equip yourself with either a second outdoor aerial, or alternatively use a small distribution amplifier with the aerial used for the main domestic set. The Labgear 6034/DA, for instance, will drive up to four sets from a single aerial. Loft or set-top aerials are unlikely to be much use unless you live in an exceptionally good reception area. The knowledge that you have a decent signal going into the set removes one doubt when fault-finding.

Your first glance into the works of a colour TV can be very daunting. There seems to be about three times as much in it than in a mono set, with a bewildering network of interconnecting leads between panels. It helps to remember that once upon a time even the mono set appeared complicated, too! On closer examination you will find that whatever the make, the set is made up of a number of sub-assemblies. The usual arrangement is as follows:

1. Tuner unit. 2. Vision and sound IF strip and Luminance amplifier. 3. Decoder. 4. Colour difference amplifiers. 5. Timebases and EHT unit. 6. Power Supply. 7. Convergence unit. 8. C.R.T. and its ancillaries.

It is beyond the scope of this book to give a detailed technical description of the PAL colour system. However, as it is essential that the broad principles are understood to enable fault-finding to take place, there follows a very brief guide.

A colour television picture is built up from three primary colours – red, green and blue. The picture tube has three "gun" assemblies, one for each colour, and on the inside of the viewing screen are groups of phosphor dots, again in threes. To ensure that the red gun, for instance, illuminates only the red dots, and so on, just behind the dots is a device called the shadow-mask. This has over 400,000 holes, through which the stream of electrons from each gun has to pass; by careful design and subsequent adjustment of certain controls the registration of the colours can be made almost perfect. But how do we get these three colours from the transmitted signal?

The tuner unit and IF amplifier stages of the colour TV are very similar to those in a mono set, especially as regards the sound. But instead of there being a "video" output as in the black-and-white set, we have a luminance amplifier at the end. This works in much the same way as a video amplifier by varying the brightness of the image on the three screens.

Contained within the luminance signal is the chrominance, or colour information, transmitted in the supressed sideband mode. Readers who are keen short-wave fans will know how a local oscillator (BFO) has to be used in a radio receiver to decode the otherwise meaningless single-side-band transmissions. A similar system operates in a colour TV, but here the local oscillator has a very precise frequency – 4.43361875 mHz to be exact – so a crystal control is used. Even this is not sufficient to maintain accuracy, so it is locked to the incoming signal by what is called the burst gate. Extracting the burst of colour information which follows the line sync pulses, it operates as does the familiar flywheel sync in a mono TV. The burst gate has to have a switching pulse applied to it, normally derived from a winding on the line output transformer.

We must now return to the chroma signal, which is amplified by usually two transistor stages. The input to the second stage is controlled by the saturation or "colour" control. The chroma signal passes on to a delay line, in which it is separated into two distinct channels, U and V. These two each have their own synchronous detector, but they operate in different ways. To understand this we have to consider the reference oscillator once more. Its output is taken virtually directly to the U detector, but it has to be continuously phase-reversed before being coupled to the V stage. It is this phase reversal which distinguishes the PAL (Phase Alternate Line) system from the original American N.T.S.C., and which gives it its immunity from changes of hue. The phase reversal is accomplished by a pair of diodes driven by a form of multi-vibrator known as a bi-stable. This in turn is controlled by a 7.8 kHz signal (half line frequency) again derived from the line output transformer.

The U and V detectors produce, respectively, the blue and red colour difference signals, which are passed on to the colour difference amplifiers. The green signal is derived from the other two signals, either before or after amplification. The luminance information may be injected into either the amplifiers or directly into the picture tube.

Another feature of all colour sets is the "colour killer". This detects the presence or otherwise of colour information; when it is absent the killer disables the chroma amplifiers, thus preventing spurious colours appearing on monochrome transmissions.

The sync seperator and time bases of the colour set are similar in most respects to those used for mono, but the higher powers required to scan the colour tube necessitates larger output transformers. Various waveforms derived from the line and frame time bases are used to provide control of convergence, i.e., to ensure that registration of the three colours on the tube face are indeed perfect, as was mentioned earlier. This process will be described in more detail later in the book.

Power supplies are provided, in most hybrid sets, by conventional use of silicon rectifiers and resistance/capacity or inductance/capacity smoothing, for both high and low voltage. It is this relative simplicity which makes them more attractive to the amateur than the highly stabilised – and complicated – units employed in all-transistor sets.

The above is a highly simplified description of colour TV workings, particularly as regards the decoder stage. As we deal with this, and the rest of the stages in the step-by-step fault finding guide, a more detailed examination of the circuitry will be given. Chapters three, four, and five will deal with power supplies; Line and frame time bases; and tuner/I.F./luminance panels respectively. Their object will be to restore picture and sound to a previously "dead" set, even if this results only in a monochrome picture for the time being. Chapter six will deal with tracing loss of colour, and subsequent chapters will cover adjustments such as purity and convergence, and obtaining spare parts. Hopefully, this will eventually lead to your having very acceptable colour pictures which are (nearly) "all your own work"!

Service Sheets. These are, of course, essential for fault-finding and setting up the convergence, etc. Manufacturers' own publications are usually restricted to the trade, but various specialist firms offer their own manuals for around 50p each. The names of these firms are to be found in the advertisement columns of relevant magazines.

Spare Parts. The various sources of supply are dealt with in detail later on in this book.

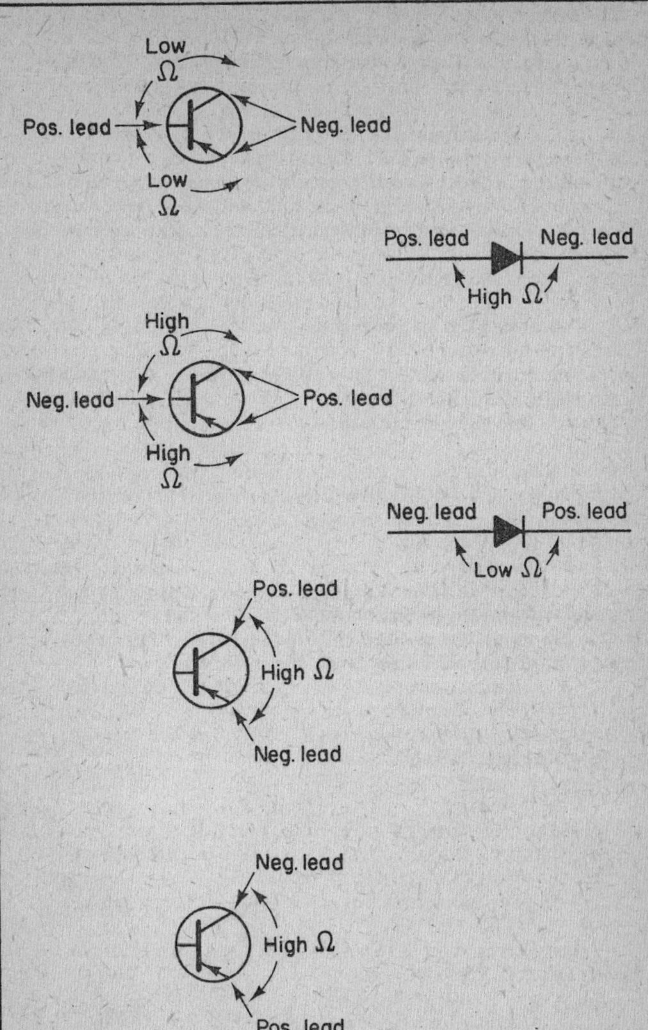

Quick tests for semiconductors using the Multi-meter.
Please refer to page 22

Using the Quick Check Chart for Semiconductors

Diodes and transistors may be tested very simply by measuring the internal resistances with a test-meter. The principle is that between certain connections there should be a high resistance when the meter leads are applied in one way, and a low resistance in another. Additionally, transistors should also exhibit a high resistance between collector and emitter, irrespective of the meter connections. The chart shows the tests for diodes and P-N-P transistors. For N-P-N types the meter leads are applied in the opposite polarity, e.g., positive to collector, negative to base.

An extension of these tests is to determine the polarity of unmarked diodes and transistors.

Important Note. The tests hold good for meters in which the positive of the internal battery is connected to the positive test lead. This is not always so, and this should be determined either by tracing through or the use of another meter on a low d.c. range. When the polarity is found to be reversed it is a good plan to stick a label onto the meter saying something like "Reverse meter leads for transistor checks", in order to remind yourself.

No actual resistance values are quoted, as these are dependent to a large extent on the device under test and the meter in use. Always switch to the lowest range, as typical values lie within the 5-200 ohm range. Dead shorts instead of low resistances will show up readily if the meter has a low range of say 0-1000 ohms.

CHAPTER THREE

Power Supply Stages

It is a curious fact that the radio industry of this country seems to unlearn a lot of experience each time it creates a new product for the domestic market. In the early days of mains radios the h.t. voltage was dropped by power resistors to several various levels, each being decoupled by its own smoothing capacitor. After many years it became clear that these elaborate arrangements were unnecessary, and the number of capacitors reduced to perhaps one double or treble unit. But as soon as television receivers appeared, the industry went straight back to the complex smoothing circuits again. In due course television h.t. supplies were simplified, until colour TV came on the scene, when once again history was repeated....! Which explains why some of the early sets had numerous h.t. lines – for instance the Philips G6 had no fewer than 9 positive rails, plus one – 24v supply! Fortunately not all sets were quite as well-endowed, but in any event even the G6 could not be as complex as the Thorn 2000 and later 3000 chassis, which had very elaborate stabilising circuits needed for transistor line output stages.

The typical power stage for a hybrid set has a small mains transformer which supplies 6.3 volts for the tube heater, and 20-30v for the low voltage line. The latter may have either full-wave or bridge rectification, with quite large values of smoothing capacitors, commonly up to 4000uf. The associated smoothing resistors are not likely to exceed 100 ohms.

The high voltage line is usually derived from the mains via a low value (5-10 ohms) limiting resistor and silicon rectifier, such as the BY127. Certain makers, such as Philips, again in their G6, preferred to split the load between two rectifiers, each with its own limiting resistor. In the case of the G6, the latter resistors were associated with thermal fuses, which opened up if excess current caused them to overheat. GEC, on the other hand, fitted a thermistor in series with the fixed limiting resistor, to prevent a large surge of voltage when the set was switched on from cold. There was no HT fuse as such; the entire set was protected by just one 3 amp. fuse in the mains supply lead to the on/off switch. In later models, however, an overload cut-out was fitted in the line output stage to protect the transformer and valves. The outward sign of its presence is a small red button protruding through a hole in the chassis at its extreme bottom right, looking at the rear view. Obviously it is a good plan to try to determine what was the cause of its operating before re-setting.

The valve heaters are invariably series-run, often, but not always, with a silicon rectifier as part of the voltage-dropping circuit. Sets with tapped primary mains transformers (e.g., Baird, Decca) generally take the heater supply from the 200v tapping, to reduce the amount of power wasted in the dropper. The use of thermistors to prevent switching-on surges is again not universal, even though it would appear to be a desirable feature.

Another item associated with the power unit is the degaussing coils which are fitted around the c.r.t. They are fed with a.c. from the mains via a positive-co-efficient thermistor – i.e., one whose resistance increases when hot. In practice this takes place very quickly indeed, so that current flows through the coils for just a few seconds when the set is switched on, either from cold, or after a rest of about five minutes or more. The B.R.C.2000 chassis also automatically degaussed when changing from 405 to 625 lines, and vice versa, provided that this was not done at intervals of less than 3-5 minutes.

Fault-finding in Power Supply Stages

The first step must be to check the following:

1. Is the set completely dead, i.e. no valve or tube heaters alight, no sound. (In the case of sets with transistor audio stages)
2. Tube heaters alight, but no valves. Otherwise as above.
3. Valves and tube lit, no sound or picture.
4. Sound absent, or picture absent.

Or, of course, a combination of some of the above.

If you have managed to obtain a service sheet for your set you will be able to see at once if the sound is produced by a valve or transistors. Otherwise refer to the table on page 15. Transistorised sound is very handy here, as it provides an audible check on whether or not the low-voltage line is functioning. Fairly obviously, the presence of low voltage indicates that the mains are reaching the set, and the transformer. In this case the tube heaters should be lit, but failure to do so may be due merely to bad contacts on the base, or on the wiring to it. You would be very unlikely to have the bad luck to find the heaters open circuit. Cross-check by reading the a.c. voltage across pins 1 and 14 of the tube base. If only the tube heaters are unlit, the rest of the set should be starting to work, so beware of high voltages on the focus pin!

Utter silence and lack of heaters is quite possibly due to a blown mains fuse, but have a good look at a faulty one before throwing it in the bin. A small break in the wire, with no discolouration of the glass, is often the result of a gradual overload, such as would be caused by the line output stage drawing heavy current under fault conditions. Should the inside of the fuse be completely blackened, however, it points to a sudden and catastrophic overload. Common causes are the failure of the mains suppression capacitor, or the h.t. rectifier. Always check the resistance from the fuseholder to chassis before fitting another fuse. The minimum resistance recorded should be that of the mains transformer primary, and/or degaussing coils. Even though these will read very low, they will be distinguished from a dead short on (say) the ohms divided by 100 range of an AVO 8, or its equivalent. Be warned that the plastic-sealed capacitors commonly used from mains to chassis frequently heal themselves after a flash-over, and may read quite o.k. on a meter. This can happen several times before the final self-destruction. The only real test to be made domestically is to connect a suspected capacitor across the mains in series with a 100w light bulb, and to wait for the latter to light up!

There is always a temptation to merely snip out a failed capacitor, and not to replace it; this is not really recommended, as any curious spiky pulses which may appear on the mains will be free to enter the set and upset the rectifiers.

Testing from fuse to earth may not reveal an h.t. short, so test directly across the rectifier. It should have a low resistance one way, and quite high the other. Exactly similar readings point to failure here. Reading from the h.t. line to earth in the usual manner, i.e., with the negative meter lead clipped on the chassis, is also misleading; a short will probably be registered due to a path through the rectifier and mains transformer. Reversing the meter leads should give the familiar needle-hard-over, backing-off-slowly effect. Again, similar readings indicate trouble. Experience suggests that the main smoothing capacitors seldom go dead short, and that this type of fault is mostly due to a smaller-value component further down the line. This has to be traced by methodically disconnecting leads to the h.t. supply until the short disappears, or in some cases reading across various points from h.t. to earth with the meter to determine the place at which the resistance is lowest. In practice this often boils down to high-voltage capacitors in the line circuit, in particular those of around 150-200 pF which are frequently to be found connected between the cathode of the boost diode and earth. The second favourite is the plastic-sealed type of capacitor of 0.1-0.47 uF, also to be found in and around the line stage.

Tracing h.t. shorts is aided in sets with an h.t. fuse, as this can be removed to isolate part of the circuitry.

A fault which is fairly common is the failure of the thermistor supplying a.c. to the rectifier. The disc types come adrift where the connecting wires are fastened, causing sparks to fly when the set is switched on. The rod variety tend to split near one end, occasionally arcing across, but more often springing far enough apart to completely deaden the set.

The fixed value surge-limiting resistors used in other sets are also vulnerable; when replacing a faulty one make sure that you use one of sufficient wattage, as even with the low values commonly employed the amount of power dissipated is quite large.

Turning to the low-tension supply, the transformer itself is not likely to give trouble. The rectifier(s) are probably the chief candidates for inspection here; the ohmeter will soon tell you if a short has taken place, or if part of a bridge has gone open circuit. Decca, by the way, used a separate rectifier for the 26 volt supply to the audio stage, in later versions of their dual-standard sets. This component, a BY234, seems to have a fairly large failure rate. It generally goes dead short, announcing this by causing a powerful hum in the loud-speaker. If you don't happen to have a low-voltage rectifier handy to replace the BY234, a BY100 will work well enough.

It will be appreciated that the smoothing of the l.t. line is vitally important, but again over the years the capacitors employed have proved to be remarkably reliable, even when subjected to a.c. following a rectifier failure. Incidentally, the supply is frequently arranged to be both positive and negative as regards earth, with the latter the mid point. This entails having two lots of smoothing, with some of the capacitors' positive terminals connected to earth. You need to bear this in mind if you do have to replace one, and be sure either to use an insulated type, or alternatively wrap a layer of tape around a plain metal can.

The heater chain starts in the power stage with its droppers and/or thermistors. The former seldom give trouble, as they are not so highly stressed as in mono. sets. (They have fewer volts to drop and consequently dissipate less power), but the latter are subject to the same kind of failure experienced in the h.t. supply. Strictly speaking, most heater faults do not lie in the power pack at all, but it is more convenient to deal with them here. High on the list is valve failure, either by open circuiting, or by shorting from heater to cathode. An undetected h/k short lasting more than a few minutes can lead to trouble in other valves, as they are forced to take more than their fair share of heater volts. Always check to see if all the valves are lit if some seem extremely bright. It's common practice to insert small decoupling capacitors at various parts of the heater chain, and these too can fail, giving the same effect as a heater/cathode short.

Other causes of over-bright heaters are (a) a short on the heater rectifier, where used, and (b) a wrong value of dropping resistor having been fitted. It's definitely a good idea to check replacements, as some engineers are not always too fussy in this respect.

Degaussing coils just don't fail! They are robustly constructed and, after all, are actively employed for only minutes in a year. It is possible to have them out of action for quite a long time without noticing any ill-effect on the screen, until and unless someone inadvertantly brings a magnet into close contact with it! Should the odd-coloured patches produced not disappear next time the set is switched on from cold, the most likely explanation is an open-circuit thermistor. These closely resemble the familiar ones in the heater and h.t. line, but possess, of course, a positive temperature co-efficient. The replacement must be of the same type, or the de-gaussing coils will go out in a blaze of glory!

Discussion of the Thorn 2000 power supply/regulator units, which are completely unlike anything used in hybrid sets, has deliberately been left to the end of the chapter. Anyone intent upon repairing these items, rather than replacing the complete panels, will find that a detailed service manual is absolutely essential. Briefly, the mains input is to a transformer, whose primary is adjustable in 10 volt steps from 200 to 250 volts. There are four secondary windings, delivering respectively 55, 68, 235, and 6.3 volts, the last for the tube heater. Each of the other windings feeds a bridge rectifier and extensive resistance-capacity smoothing networks. The power supply board also carries a beam current limiting transistor for the c.r.t., and a regulator transistor for the 66 volt line.

Current from the power board passed to a regulator panel employing three transistors for the frame time base supply, and two for that to the line time base. A further two transistors form what is called an electronic trip. This cuts off the voltage on the line time base in the event of surges which could cause damage. In normal circumstances it is only necessary to switch the set off for half a minute or so to effect restoration of working; should no picture then appear there is a persistent fault which must be investigated.

Obviously, even such a complex panel as this is repairable, but the snag as far as the enthusiast is concerned is that the high power transistors used are rather expensive, and it is all too easy for one of these to "blow" again, should the initial fault remain untraced. Hence the advantage of having a spare panel which can either be used as a direct replacement if in good condition, or alternatively stripped for parts. In cases of real difficulty there are various specialist firms who will recondition panels. They can usually be found in the advertisement columns of TV servicing periodicals.

CHAPTER FOUR

Time Bases

It was remarked earlier in this book that the time bases of a colour TV differ but little from those of mono. sets. In the case of the frame time base the main difference is that most manufacturers abandoned the single valve oscillator/output arrangement in favour of a separate oscillator driving a PL508 output pentode. This has a power rating more suitable for the work of scanning a colour tube. The oscillator is nearly always an ECC82, the exceptions being Baird(PCF80) and Philips (ECC81).

Pye group sets use a transistorised oscillator and output stage. It is a small panel which has the twin virtues of simplicity and reliability. The circuitry is very similar to that of the Thorn 2000, but in this latter case the frame time base shares a panel with the audio amplifier and output transistors.

Line time bases have three valves common to all hybrids, namely, PCF802 oscillator, PL509 output, PY500 boost diode. Sets employing valve EHT rectifiers and/or stabilers employ the GY501 and PD500. The focus potential of around 5kV can be obtained by various means. It may be bled from the main e.h.t. by a network of high-value resistors, or rectified separately, either by a silicon type, or a valve. Bush used a DY87 for the job, while Philips went so far as to resurrect the EY51, veteran of mono. TV since the early post-war days! Sets with solid-state triplers invariably have a tapping on this unit to give the focus voltage.

Another feature of the pioneer black-and-white sets had to be reintroduced after a long period of disuse. This is the electronic shift control system for picture centreing. The magnetic shift controls used on the neck of mono. tubes cannot be used for colour, as it would interfere with the purity magnets to be found in this position, so it was back to the old method! This entails having a small amount of d.c. passing through the scan coils, controlled by a low-value variable resistor, commonly 50-100 ohms. A means is normally provided of reversing the polarity of the current in case the picture should be too far over one way even at maximum on the control.

In addition to actually scanning the c.r.t. the time bases provide the combinations of waveforms necessary to "converge" the three guns. As it is a unit in its own right, the convergence panel will be dealt with in a later chapter.

Fault-finding, 1. Valve Line Stages

The first thing to be tried when the line output fails is, of course, the valves. When the PY500 is seen to be glowing red hot on its anode it could be due to an internal short, or more likely to the breaking-down of a capacitor. (See under power supplies for details.) These valves are also prone to suddenly giving up all emission, resulting in zero volts on the PL509 anode. If this latter is overheating one naturally hopes that it is due to lack of drive from the oscillator, but there is always the fear that the line output transformer could have gone. The preliminary check is to see if there is a good negative voltage on the control grid, absence of which would certainly point to the oscillator stage. Again, replacement of the PCF802 valve is the favourite.

Having pinned the fault down to either oscillator or output, you can now start detailed checks. Assuming that drive is present at the grid of the PL509, try the old trick of running the set with the PY500 top cap removed. This will restore partial operation where the boost capacitor has gone dead short, or will alternatively prevent the PL509 from overheating by removing its anode voltage, a useful consideration when testing is likely to take a fair time. The snag here is that lack of anode voltage causes the screen grid to be greedy, and to run its supply resistor hot, so keep an eye on it. It must be mentioned here that this component can stop the line output stage dead should it go open circuit. Also examine all the ancillary components mounted on and around the line transformer, especially those subjected to high peak voltages. Remove the lead from the transformer to the voltage tripler, as this component has been known to develop internal shorts. Replace the top cap on the PY500 and check with a neon tester on the PL509 anode for flyback volts. If there is still no life, it's just possible that there could be a fault on the scan coils or the convergence network. These are normally connected by plugs and sockets, so it is reasonably easy to exonerate them or otherwise. If all else fails to provide the answer then, reluctantly, the transformer must be blamed. Over the years service engineers have always had to face up to this problem of replacing what is the most expensive item in a set after the tube, since this is the one certain way of proving that the original one is faulty.

As replacements tend to be quite costly – around £10 – this is another instance in which having a spare set handy is invaluable.

Whilst on the subject, it must be noted that line transformers can cause other problems even when they are operating correctly as far as scanning the tube is concerned. The numbers of subsidiary windings producing pulses for the decoder, etc., can go open circuit, giving the effect of no colour, or perhaps incorrect colours. This is a very annoying state of affairs, since the "expensive" part of the transformer is quite o.k. and it could be well worth the enthusiast's time to attempt rewinding bad sections.

Replacement transformers are obtainable from the manufacturers service departments only through authorised dealers. There are, however, specialist firms who wind their own spares, and supply them to the public via the advertisements in TV journals. Before purchasing from such firms it is strongly recommended that you ascertain that theirs is an exact replacement. Some need to have parts from the old transformer transferred over, and this can be a tedious and lengthy proceeding. It may also be found that the fixing lugs, etc., do not match up properly, and that it is impossible to remount the tripler, for instance. A genuine spare is then worth the small extra cost!

Returning to the oscillator stage, it's probably fair to say that about 90% of failures are due to valve trouble. The remainder will be resistor and capacitor faults, with shorted turns on the oscillator transformer as the outside chance. Voltage checks on the valve should soon enable you to trace component failures.

From time to time you may encounter loss of sync., with the picture either running in lines, or "floating" across the screen. The discriminator diodes are the likely cause of this, and as colour TVs are bristling with diodes, do make sure you have the right ones before replacing! In many cases there will be one of the small dual units which have been a familiar sight in mono. sets for a number of years. These may be replaced by a couple of good silicon diodes, such as the 1N914.

2. Valve Frame Stages

When initially testing a set, and confronted by a single line across the screen you should not automatically start fault-finding on the frame time base. Some sets were fitted with a switch which collapses the frame for grey-scale adjustments; it's possible that this may inadvertently have been operated. Moving on from this, the PL508 is your next item on the check list. When a replacement restores frame scan, cast your eyes around the panel in its vicinity in case any component appears to have suffered when the original valve failed. The bias resistor in particular should be measured to ensure that it retains its correct value.

A fault on the oscillator stage may result in either complete loss of scan, or reduced height, or a false lock (wrong speed). All three are often attributable to resistors which have changed their value. Ones to look out for are high-resistance types feeding h.t. from the boost line to the driver part of the oscillator, and those in series with the hold control. The multi-vibrator is employed in most sets, with the exception of Baird; the anode of the first section is fed by a resistor of 22k-100k ohms, another component worth testing. When fitting a replacement here it will pay to use a rather higher wattage type than the original.

When loss of frame sync. is experienced, suspect the inverter or limiter which is usually interposed between the sync. seperator and the oscillator. It may be either a diode or triode, in the latter case one section of a valve such as a PCF80 or ECC82.

3. Transistor Frame Stages

Both examples of this, Pye and Thorn, employ a blocking oscillator/driver/output sequence, the last being a pair of BD124s. The general design is extremely straightforward and unlikely to give much trouble. The output transistors do sometimes burn out, possibly the victims of the "domino" effect common to many transistor oscillator/amplifier arrangements. (When the first in the chain fails, the others follow). You will probably end up changing all four transistors. Electrolytic capacitors can be the cause of loss of height or linearity when aging reduces their values. Check by connecting a good one in parallel. The 250 uf which couples the output pair to the scan coils is always worth trying if the raster is badly cramped.

4. Transistor Line/e.h.t. Stages

By which, of course, we refer to the Thorn group products. The line time base has a reactance stage (BC107) controlling a blocking oscillator employing the same type of transistor. A 2S035 driver is transformer coupled to the output pair, twin R1039s. The e.h.t. is not derived from the line output stage, but from another unit having no fewer than 7 transistors, culminating in a single R1038 for output. The tripler delivers 24kV and 4-5kV for the tube anode and focus electrode respectively. Here are two more examples of rather complex design, for which spare transistors and transformers would be costly. Once again the best plan is to substitute complete panels when trouble arises.

Converting Valve EHT Supplies to Solid-state Triplers

Not only is the circuitry for an EHT tripler simpler than for the valve supply, it is also completely free from the X-radiation hazard which is associated with the latter. It is thus obviously desirable whenever possible to convert to a tripler. Since all tubes operate at the same nominal anode and focus potentials, the selection of a unit is not critical. The ITT-made replacement for the later single-standard GEC sets is a good choice, because of its small physical size.

Your first step will be to remove the overwind on the line output transformer which supplies the GY501 rectifier. This valve, the associated PD500, and their holders, may be removed altogether. To maintain the heater circuit at its correct current, the connecting leads to pins 4 and 5 of the PD500 should be taken to a 25 ohm 3 watt resistor, mounted on a conveniently sited tag strip.

The original focus supply will have to go, as well. This may be a small high voltage silicon rectifier or a standard EHT valve, e.g., DY86. In the latter case, the holder again is taken out. The new supply comes from a tapping on the tripler.

The tripler should be mounted in such a way that n leads is unduly close to windings on the transformer, save w tion has to be made. To let the 25kV output lead rest on t is to ask for trouble, namely, a fizz and a flash, followed by of both components.

There are always four leads on triplers. One goes to t of the PL509, one to the focus control, one to the tube anod the last to earth. In some instances the original focus control will be unsuitable. If a metrosil type is not available, a substit be made up very easily from the contents of the average works junk box. All you need is a square of paxolin measuring aroun a preset pot. of 1 – 2 megohms, and about eight 1 watt resisto 1 – 4.7 megohms. Any combination that gives a total of about megs is o.k. Initially, string all the fixed resistors end to end, fr focus supply to earth. Hook the wire from the tube to a joint a a quarter of the total resistance from earth. Switch the set on, a check the focus. You will readily find a tapping which gives reas results. Switch off, break the chain at the optimum point, and in the preset. Take the centre contact to the tube. It should now b possible to vary the voltage sufficiently to get the focus exact.

Having determined the above, make a note of how the resis were wired, and unsolder them. Lay them on the sheet of paxolin and mark with a pencil positions which will allow them a good clea ance from each other. Drill small holes to accept the end wires two a time. They must be pushed through, twisted together for a couple of turns, and "blobbed" with solder to prevent corona discharge. The preset is mounted in the appropriate place, and connected as before. If you happen to have some EHT sealer spray handy, give whole a couple of coats. Fasten the completed unit somewhere in the cabinet where it may be adjusted, but not easily touched accidentally.

Most sets have a set EHT control, and if you have means o measuring 25kV, it is as well to check that the anode volts are ne the norm. Sometimes the control has a marked effect upon the so the safest thing to do is to settle for a sharp picture/correct w combination. If sufficient width is absolutely unobtainable oth you could experiment with connecting a high voltage "pulse" c of 50 – 150 pf. between the top cap of the PY500 and earth. extreme cases you could even try from the PL509 anode to ea In both cases be sure that the capacitor is rated at minimum 1

Having removed the source of X-radiation, you may if remove or modify part of the line output can to accomodate tripler. Nevertheless, sufficient protection around the transf itself should be left, to minimise radiation of the line time b to prevent contact with high voltage points.

CHAPTER FIVE

From Tuner Unit to Luminance Amplifier

All but one of the sets we have to consider was fitted with a push-button UHF tuner unit. The exception was the Baird 700 series. At the time of its production, there was of course only the one station available on UHF, and so the disadvantages of the rotary tuner were probably not immediately obvious. It would be possible to modify the set to take a push-button unit without having to drill the cabinet. In cases like this the new unit may be screwed to the top rear of the cabinet so that just the knobs appear above it. Almost any make of tuner is suitable, the only consideration being whether it was intended for positive HT line, as was the original.

Decca, Bush, Philips, Pye, and Thorn all had 6-button integrated tuners covering VHF and UHF. In most cases these may be adjusted to operate on UHF only. GEC and ITT had four-button UHF tuners, and in the former case mechanical wear can cause erratic operation after years of use. The usual symptoms are failure to tune accurately when switched from one station to another, and drift when left on one particular channel. Cleaning the contact springs which earth the variable capacitor in the unit, and subsequent smearing with silicon grease can mitigate this trouble, but in the long term replacement is the only real answer. The GEC tuner unit bears a strong resemblance to that used in the Philips TG170 series of black-and-white sets, suggesting a fruitful and inexpensive source of spares.

All types of tuners are at risk during electrical storms, even when actual lightning strikes may occur quite long distances away. The RF amplifier transistor is the usual victim, which can be checked by connecting the aerial, via a small capacitor, to a point somewhere near the second transistor's base. The exact spot is not crucial, and you should soon discover a place where the signal is received reasonably well. If the resulting picture is better than that received through the aerial socket, first measure the voltages on the RF transistor before attempting to replace it – just in case another component should have failed. Note that manufacturers sometimes changed the type of tuner unit during production runs, so select a replacement transistor equivalent to the one removed, rather than by relying on the circuit diagram to be correct. (The most likely difference is the use of silicon in place of germanium transistors.) Take extreme care when unsoldering the faulty transistor not to bend the wiring or tuning bars, as this could lead to difficulties in getting all three channels to tune in properly. The same applies, of course, when fitting the new transistor, and in addition it is suggested that the lead wires should be held with a pair of fine-nosed pliers to act as a heat sink during soldering.

Much of the above applies also to the oscillator transistor, but in this case it is not possible to treat by the aerial method, only by metering and/or substitution.

The small disc capacitors widely used in tuner units can split apart, but so slightly as to not be immediately noticed. These are well worth checking when the transistors appear to be blameless.

The three or four trimming capacitors mounted on the side of many units should not be adjusted unless absolutely essential. This would mainly occur when (a) the fitting of a new component has upset the alignment, or (b) if the trimmers have previously been disturbed. As may be imagined, to re-align a tuner unit properly, very accurate signal generators have to be used. However a very fair attempt may be made, as follows:

Tune to the middle channel of your local group, which in most cases is ITV. Adjust the trimmer nearest to the oscillator section for sound and vision to appear together. Peak up the rest of the trimmers, not favouring vision at the expense of sound, or vice-versa. Then tune to the other channels to see if they too come in correctly. Re-adjust the trimmers very slightly if necessary to achieve balance. Finally, the IF output coil should be gently adjusted, again for a good balance of sound and picture. This is best done whilst watching a test card, to obtain the best bandwidth, as registered by the vertical gratings on either side of the centre circle. Ideally, even the finest should be sharp, but in practice this is not always possible.

Although the IF strip will be of the dual-standard type, for our purpose we can ignore the 405-line components. Indeed, in some cases it may be possible to solder the system switch in its 625 position, thus eliminating any potential trouble due to bad contacts.

The intercarrier sound system, whereby the latter's IF is tapped off just before or after the vision detector, gives a useful cross-checking facility. If sound is present, but not vision, the fault must lie after the take-off point. Alternatively, when both have disappeared, the fault will lie in the IF strip itself (or the tuner unit, of course).

To check the sound IF amplifiers, normally all that is needed is to put a meter prod on the input. This acts as an aerial and will pick up short-wave station on the 49 metre band, if all is well. If no sound at all results, try the effect of lightly tapping the meter prod, switched to ohms, on the centre tap of the volume control. This should produce loud clicks in the speaker. Having narrowed down the field in this way, you can procede with checking individual stages.

Measure the voltages on suspect transistors. Even if the correct values are not quoted on the service sheet, the conventional arrangement of the base having slightly more voltage than the emitter, and the collector not far off that of the HT rail, will normally hold good as a basis for tests. Unusual voltage readings should be followed up by the standard base-emitter, base collector resistance checks. BF194 transistors in particular seem prone to failure due to internal shorts. The BF115, an excellent multi-purpose RF transistor, acts as a replacement here, as in many other applications. In some cases it will be found that the printed board is drilled to take the fourth (earthing) lead of the BF115; otherwise it may be bent up out of the way and left unconnected.

Some engineers seem to have a fair amount of trouble with small capacitors, notably the semi-transparent plastic variety, but this has not been the author's experience. Nevertheless, these may be suspected in the event of unstability, or radical lack of gain even with new transistors.

The mere replacement of a transistor in the vision or sound IF strip should not have any marked effect upon the alignment, provided that surrounding components are disturbed as little as possible.

Whilst on this subject, a few words of caution concerning realignment. It should not, in fact, be necessary throughout the working life of the set in normal circumstances, due to the inherent stability of transistor IF amplifiers. It follows the mis-alignment should be suspected only when all other causes of poor performance have been discounted, or, as with the tuner, it is obvious that it has been interfered with. A "smeary" picture, for instance can be the result of a component failure around the luminance amplifier, such as the anode and cathode resistors and by-pass capacitors. Grainy pictures are seldom due to faults on the IF stages – the tuner unit is a much more likely suspect. Separation of sound and vision, with both weak, can also be traced to this. Low signal strength can give the same effect.

On the sound side, a background buzz can be due to misalignment, but might well be caused by poor smoothing of the HT or LT supply. Another prime suspect is the 50Hz frame pulses being picked up by a badly routed or unscreened AF lead.

A small balancing pot. is usually included in the sound detector circuit, and it has been known for the centre tap to cease contacting the track. This will cause quite loud buzzing, particularly on certain camera shots.

N.B. This above mentioned effect, known as "caption buzz" is very difficult to eradicate in some sets, even when perfectly aligned. The balancing control should be set for minimum buzz, preferably when there is a caption on the screen, but no sound, as sometimes occurs during a break between programmes or commercials.

If after all this, realignment proves to be called for, you should aim to beg, borrow, or otherwise obtain a signal generator and to follow the manufacturers recommended procedure. Unfortunately this latter is not always to be found in service manuals, and some kind of compromise has to be achieved. One constant is the alignment of the sound IFs to 6.0mHz, so this should be your first task. There are commonly five cores to be adjusted – one on the take-off coil near the vision detector, and four on the actual transformers. The signal generator input is to the base of the last transistor prior to the sound take-off.

Two precautions must be taken at this point. Firstly, you must equip yourself with a correctly fitting tool with which to adjust the cores. Failure to do this will almost certainly result in splitting one or more of them, entailing hours of tedious and painstaking work in removing the broken bits. The correct tool for most small cores is a moulded hard plastic handle having non-ferrous blades of two different sizes set into its ends. The blades will pass through the length of the core, greatly reducing the tendency to split. Larger cores often have a hexagonal hole down the centre instead of a screwdriver slot. The proper tool has one end fashioned part hexagonal, part round, so that it may be slipped through the top core of a pair to adjust the lower.

Whichever type you need should be available for a few pence at components dealers.

Secondly, the signal generator must be isolated from the transistors by capacitors of about 0.01uf, 1000vw. This is to positively prevent any stray voltages from entering the set and causing damage. Mains operated generators frequently have capacitors connected from both sides of the mains lead to chassis, to by-pass any unwanted RF, and should one of these "leak" enough voltage could pass through it to ruin a transistor. In addition there may in fact be a slight potential difference between the neutral main and earth, so that even with the set connected correctly to the mains, there could again be that nasty little voltage between it and the generator. Better be safe than sorry!

Having connected the generator to the TV, set it to give 6.0mHz, modulated, and tune the sound IF transformers for maximum. The final core tunes the ratio detector, and this must subsequently be reset on a signal for minimum distortion and buzz.

Once the sound channel is known to be reasonably on tune, the generator output should be taken to the point where the tuner input enters the set. The tuning should be swung slowly over the range 30-38 mHz, through most of which bars should be seen on the screen. It is unlikely that the alignment would be so far out to prevent some sort of signal passing through. If maker's instructions are available follow them closely. This often involves the use of damping resistors across certain coils, batteries to simulate the effects of AGC, and so on; it is virtually impossible to give any sort of standard procedure. The best that can be done is to wait until one of the channels is transmitting test card "F", and to work from that. Since the sound must be on tune now, the tuner can be set to give this. The vision should come into tune automatically, but if it is out, as shown by poor responce of the vertical gratings, the vision cores may be gently altered, keeping a close eye on the screen. Settings should be found where the best bandwidth, consistent with good sound, is available. This means that at least the first five of the six gratings should be sharply defined. Under good conditions the sixth should also be visible.

At this stage the colour information ought to be received satisfactorily, and provided that everything else is in order the colours should spring up in the centre circle. Final slight readjustments must be made to eliminate objectionable patterning on the colours.

Sometimes the bandwidth gratings will exhibit a kind of herring-bone effect, but this is not of any consequence and may be ignored.

Sound-on-vision interference is far less likely to occur than with 405-line IF strips, but any slight trouble here may normally be dealt with quite easily. The 6.0mHz sound take off coil frequently doubles as a rejector for the vision detector, and should be set to give the minimum patterning on screen, rather than maximum sound.

It must be emphasised that this "rule of thumb" method of alignment must be regarded as for emergency use only, when all else fails. If satisfactory results just cannot be obtained it will pay you to return the IF panel to the makers, or a specialist repairer, with instructions that it be realigned or replaced, whichever would be more economical.

The detector stage of the vision IF strip is similar to that of a mono. TV, with added filtering to remove the chrominance information, which would otherwise cause a dot pattern to appear on the screen.

There will probably be two luminance pre-amplifiers after the detector, one of which may be an emitter-follower. The contrast control normally operates in this area. Here too will be found the luminance delay line. This particular component is necessary to compensate for the delay to the chrominance signal inherent in the PAL design. Without a corresponding delay in the luminance information, it would reach the screen slightly in advance of the colour, and cause strange effects. Physically the luminance delay line resembles a ferrite aerial, wound from end to end. They seldom give trouble, but it has been known for there to be a bad soldered joint where the windings are attached to the conductor wires. Its position in circuit varies from make to make, but is generally between the first and final luminance amplifiers.

The initial amplification of the luminance signal is carried out by a transistor of the BF115 or similar type. There may be a phase splitter or emitter follower between this and the output stage, which in hybrids is nearly always a PL802. The circuitry is much the same as that of a monochrome set, but extra precautions are taken to blank out the line and frame flyback lines, usually involving a BC108 fed with pulses from the two timebases.

Gradual changes in the level of brightness can sometimes be traced to the PL802's emission falling as it heats up. The same is true of the PFL200, the alternative used by Baird and Philips.

A major difference from black-and-white TV lies in the method commonly used to control the picture brightness. In monochrome sets the standard arrangement for many years has been to have the c.r.t. cathode at around 100-150 volts positive by coupling it closely to the video amplifier anode, and to vary the bias on the c.r.t. grid by means of a potentiometer connected into the HT line. This would not be practicable with the triple gun assembly of a colour tube, so another means has to be found. That generally adopted is to vary the anode current, and thus the voltage, of the luminance output valve by controlling the bias on its grid. Since there are negative low tension lines in most sets, the brightness control is often a low value pot. with an effective range of only a few volts. This explains why these controls appear to have a limited effect compared with those of a monochrome set. In addition, the DC component is likely to be well de-coupled to chassis by an electrolytic capacitor, resulting in a curious delayed action in certain sets whereby there is a noticeable time lag between operation of the control and alteration of the picture.

Since the range of the brightness control is so limited, it is common to find a preset added to the circuitry to give extra adjustment. Nevertheless, when the main control fails to give sufficient control it is better to look for a cause, rather than to immediately alter the preset.

Another feature associated with the luminance amplifier is the provision of variation of drive to the three guns. This may be achieved by the use of preset contrbls, or by a series of fixed tapping points (GEC). The red gun normally receives full drive, but may in some sets have an optional adjustment. (e.g. Baird). The settings for the drive controls are best found by reference to the relevant service manual, but later in this book a general guide to the procedure will be given.

Thorn Luminance Circuitry

This is actually split between two printed boards. The vision and sound IF amplifiers and detectors being on one, and the luminance amplifier and emitter follower on another, with the three colour difference amplifiers, etc. In addition the sound output stage shares a board with the frame time base. The design is pretty straight-forward, with conventional transistors. The output, for instance, is the ubiquitous BC107, and the emitter follower a BF115.

Both panels are extremely reliable, and servicing should present few problems. One point to bear in mind is that due to the large number of plug and socket interconnections the prospect of a bad joint or two is always there. The most likely offenders are the multi-way types of moulded nylon, in the female half of which are numbers of small connector sleeves, semi-floating. They are intended to press home over the male pins when the plug is inserted, but due to the construction it is possible for the sleeves to push back and to make minimal contact. The answer is to push each one gently but firmly with a fine-bladed screwdriver, until it is well seated. It can be rather surprising on occasion to see just how far the sleeves can be moved!

The edge connectors also used extensively in Thorn sets do not give much trouble, at least as far as low-voltage applications are involved. Where there is a considerable potential difference between adjacent contacts it is advisable to keep them clean. Dust etc., could conduct and eventually cause a carbon track to develop.

CHAPTER SIX

The Colour Decoder

The decoder is by far the most complicated section of the colour receiver, as even a cursory inspection will reveal. Nevertheless, a logical approach will enable you to localise and trace most faults without too much trouble.

To understand how a fault can be pinned down to a particular part of the decoder, it is necessary to take a rather more detailed look at its operation than in Chapter Two. Otherwise many of the terms which have to be used will be meaningless. On page 45 appears a block diagram of a typical decoder. Study this in conjunction with the following technical description. It may well appear bewildering at first, with the various signal paths criss-crossing, and sometimes apparently doubling back upon themselves. So initially let us consider just that part of the diagram within the red box.

The first Chroma. amplifier receives the composite video signal, i.e., the colour information and the "burst" which follows each line sync. pulse. The burst is not required to pass through the complete chroma. circuit, and so a blanking pulse from the line transformer is applied to eliminate it. Between the first and second chroma amps. is the saturation or "colour" control, which is in essence just a gain control for the second amp. The signal passes to the delay line via a driver transistor which is likely to be a BC108. The delay line splits the colour information into the "U" and "V" components, which when demodulated will provide, respectively, the blue and red drives to the colour amplifiers. The green will be obtained by subtraction or addition of the other two colours. Demodulation of the colour signals requires the aid of a local oscillator, running at exactly the same frequency as the chroma signal (4.43361875mHz) and in the correct phase. To achieve this sort of accuracy is difficult enough in itself, but this is not the end of the story.

The main feature of the "PAL" system is its resistance to phase changes in the transmitted signal, which in the American NTSC system can give rise to annoying changes of hue. This is especially apparent when long-distance link-ups are involved. For instance, when the "splash-down" of an American space ship was televised live some years ago, the sailors on the mother ship appeared to have green uniforms! In the PAL system the phase of the line is reversed constantly, hence Phase Alternate Line, which provides the initials. Errors can still enter the signal, but due to the rapid phase reversal they are not detected by the viewer's eye, and present no problem.

Having said earlier that the reference oscillator has to be in the correct phase as the incoming signal, it is now clear that the former has to have its phase reversed in step with the latter. So now we move on to the circuitry within the green box.

The reference oscillator has its frequency controlled by a quartz crystal. The output is taken more or less directly to the U channel, and via a phase switch to the V channel. The phase switch is a pair of diodes which are made to conduct alternatively and oppositely by the application of a square waveform of the appropriate polarity. The square waves are generated by what is termed a bi-stable multivibrator – i.e., one that can be switched from one stable state of oscillation to another. The change of phase takes place during the line fly-back period, which means that the bi-stable can very conveniently be switched by a pulse from the line output transformer. Thus: the LOPT switches the bistable, the bistable switches the phase changer, and the phase changer switches the phase of the reference oscillator input to the V channel. It is not difficult to imagine that unless all these operations are 100% accurate, the result will be chaos on the screen! Fortunately means are available to lock everything to the incoming signal, and for this we have to return to the burst pulse, which you will remember, was excluded from the chroma amplifiers by a blanking pulse, again drawn from the LOPT.

The first item in the black box is the Burst Gate. A pulse in opposite phase to that which blanks the burst from the chroma amps. admits it through the gate to a phase discrimator. Here it is compared with a sample from the reference oscillator. Any discrepancy in frequency or phase produces an error voltage, which can be used to pull the reference oscillator back into tune.

At the same time, the level of burst is directly related to the signal input, so by rectifying it with a small diode a bias voltage can be obtained which will control the chroma. amps. in a similar way to the familiar AGC found in mono. TVs. The full name of Automatic Chrominance Control is usually abbreviated to ACC.

The phase discriminator is meanwhile producing more than a control voltage for the reference oscillator. It also sends out what is now normally referred to as an "ident." (Identifying) pulse. This is a derivative of the burst, and has the same frequency and phase. When amplified it is applied to the bi-stable via a so-called steering diode, to ensure that the line by line switching is in fact locked to that of the transmitter.

There is yet one more duty for this versatile stage to perform. When a monochrome transmission is being received it is necessary to disable the chroma. amplifiers to prevent their producing spurious colours. (The effects produced are shown graphically when a programme containing both colour and monochrome material is transmitted. Certain aspects of the latter, particularly small areas of fine detail, can fool the chroma circuits into producing patches of blue.)

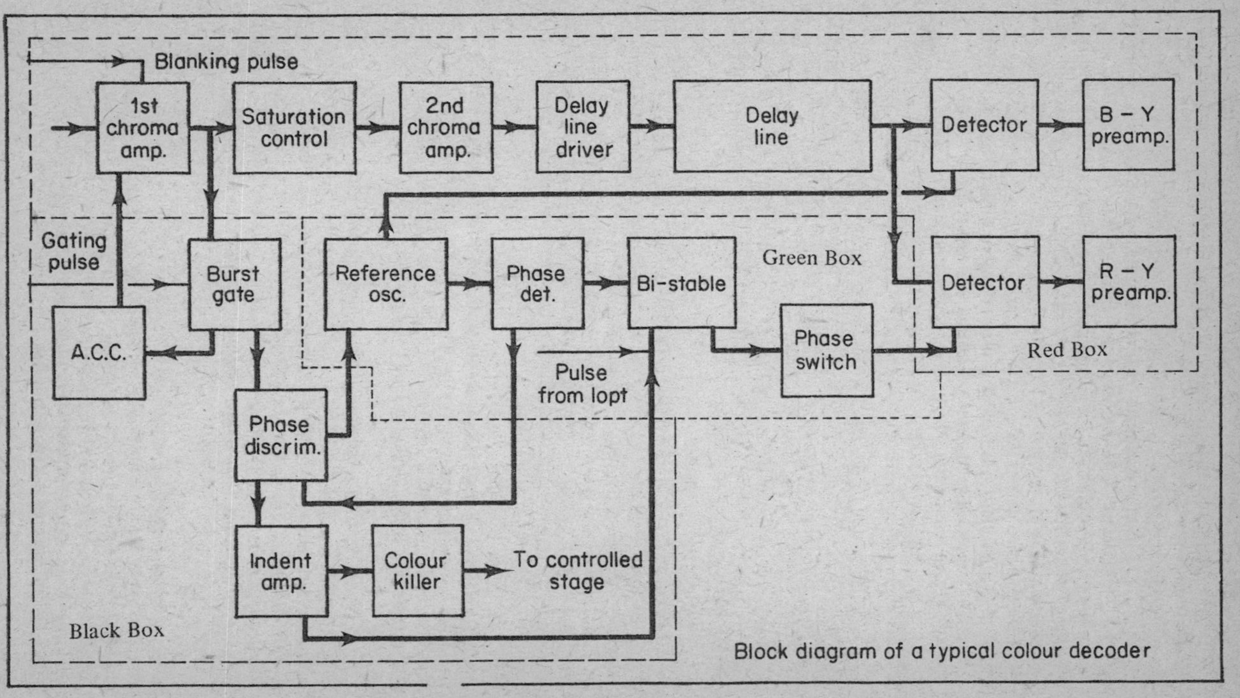

Block diagram of a typical colour decoder

Since the presence or otherwise of the burst is the certain indicator of colour or mono. transmission, the means of switching the chroma. channel on and off as required presents itself. An output from the Ident. amplifier is rectified to give a control voltage by the "colour killer". The normal system is for the controlled stage, which may be the first or second chroma amps, or the delay line driver, to be held in a biassed-off state until the necessary voltage arrives from the killer and switches it on.

It is customary to provide a preset level at which the colour killer starts to operate. A setting-up procedure for this is given later.

Detailed Fault-finding

When you are presented with a monochrome picture, which should be in colour and is not due to something as simple as mis-tuning, your first action must be to over-ride the colour killer. The precise method of doing this is usually to be found in the service manual, but generally consists of introducing bias to the controlled stage by connecting a resistor between it and the transistor HT line. This will produce one of the following three results:

A. Correct colour.
B. Incorrect or unsynchronised colour.
C. Still no colour at all.

In the case of A, the fault will lie in the killer itself. Now is the time to check if the level control is out of adjustment by turning it to either end of its travel in turn. Should this produce colour, the correct point may be found as follows:

Turn the manual colour control to maximum. Switch the set to a blank channel and remove the aerial. Look closely at the screen for the presence of colour "noise". Turn the preset to the setting where the noise just disappears. Don't go past this position.

If this is not the reason for the killer being permanently on, check all around it with the meter. The coupling to the ident amp. may be amiss, or alternatively the diode(s) in the killer rectifier could be faulty. Sometimes a d.c. amplifier transistor follows the killer to increase the bias voltage. Check that this is in order, and if so, that the coupling to the controlled stage is also ok. A systematic approach should soon reveal the cause of the trouble.

Result B calls for some deductive work. Absence of burst is the one fault which will simultaneously cause the killer to be operating continuously, and the reference oscillator and bi-stable to be out of synchronism. This condition is of course not visible on the screen until the killer is over-ridden. We must therefore look for trouble in the burst processing network and/or the reference oscillator tuning.

The first link in the chain is of course the burst gate. This is typically a pair of diodes turned "on" at the right time by the pulse from the l.o.p.t. Note that if the latter is missing the gate will be inoperative. Something as simple as a displaced plug-and-socket connection from l.o.p.t. to decoder could be responsible, but it has been known for the pulse windings to go open circuit. Check the latter with the ohm meter if in doubt. Also bear in mind the possibility of the connections on the l.o.p.t. having been made incorrectly, if this appears to have received the attention of a soldering iron recently. It is all too easy to slip up when replacing the dozen or so wires commonly attached to this component.

Another design uses a gate generator transistor which turns the burst amplifier on and off as required.

Whatever the type, check all semiconductors and small components thoroughly. Remember that unless the gate and amplifier are in order the reference oscillator and the bi-stable cannot work correctly.

If the foregoing check out correctly, move on to the phase discriminator. Here again the diodes are probably the most likely suspects. The control voltage for the reference oscillator originates here, and as with the colour killer there may be a d.c. amplifier to be investigated. Control of the oscillator is by a varactor diode, which do appear to be very reliable in service. A preset adjustment for frequency may be effected by manually varying the varactor voltage, or by a conventional small trimmer capacitor. Consult the manual before altering either type.

Faults on the oscillator stage will produce some differing effects, but at the moment we are concerned only with its not being synchronised. This will result in "rainbows" – colours swirling around, possibly in thick horizontal bars. It will *not* cause people to have green faces, nor the alternate bright and dark pairs of lines known as Hanover Blinds. These are due to the PAL switch operating, respectively, in the wrong phase or not at all. From this you should be able to narrow down the search a little more

More thought shows that the green face syndrome reveals that the bi-stable must be running, even if the phasing is wrong, so the cause must lie in the steering circuit. By the same token the PAL switch is exonerated.

Exactly the opposite applies when Hanover Blinds are encountered. Now both the bi-stable and the switch are suspect. Once again there are lots of semi-conductors to check, but my favourites here are the actual bi-stable transistors.

Here too a line pulse going astray can upset matters. so make sure of its presence.

There remains another possibility when considering incorrect colour; i.e., a synchronised picture with one primary colour obviously missing or subdued. We will assume that you have already eliminated the c.r.t. from your list of suspects! Predominate red/cyan indicates a fault in the U demodulator, the B-Y pre-amp., or the colour output valve. Excessive blue/yellow points to the V and R-Y channel.

Loss of green can be traced to the G-Y stages. Bear in mind that green is derived from the other two colours.

When dealing with the U and V demodulators, ensure that both signal and reference information is present. Bridge detectors employing four diodes each are used, in which the failure of just one will effectively stop the proceedings.

We now have to consider C-still no colour, with the killer overridden. The chroma amplifiers must be investigated, and if all seems to be well here, check the burst blanking. You will recall that one of those handy l.o.p.t. pulses eliminates the burst from the chroma channel by switching off a couple of diodes at the correct time. It follows that if the diodes should pack up, or if the pulse should be absent, then the chrominance can be lost along with the burst.

The chroma. amp. transistors can be checked conventionally. Bear in mind that a very "noisy" colour control could stop the signal from passing from one to another.

As stated earlier, the delay line driver is often a BC108 – and by now you will probably have learned to distrust these little fellows on sight, as I have!

Our next check takes us back to the reference oscillator, this time to consider its not working at all. If the transistor(s) are found to be faulty, do try to get exact replacements, as shown in the service manual. When capacitors have to be replaced, use good quality types. In the case of small capacities, close tolerance silver micas are best. Crystals have been known to fail on occasion, too.

It is to be hoped that from the above, the easily obtained impression that the decoder is a house of cards with every part interdependent, will be dispelled. A careful study of the fault condition, and a logical approach to pinning it down will in most cases result in success.

There is, of course, one very nasty eventuality which can be encountered – that a previous engineer or owner has despaired and twiddled every control and tuning core in sight. Your one great hope here is that the manufacturer marked the original settings with a dash of paint. *If* you can return everything to normal, and *if* this results in some kind of colour pictures, it is then permissible to tune for optimum performance on Test Card F. Otherwise you are on a decidedly sticky wicket. To realign a decoder "by ear" requires an enormous amount of patience and good fortune. A glance at the service manual will show just how complicated the procedure is even with the aid of sophisticated test gear. So your best bet in these circumstances is to acquire either a reconditioned or good second-hand panel.

There are now a number of independent firms offering a repair service on panels at reasonable rates. You can usually phone for a quote before comitting yourself.

In the decoder, as in most other parts of a set, there is always the chance of printed circuit faults-cracks, bad joints and the like. The double sided (GEC) panels are especially susceptible to trouble where the sole connection between one side and the other may be just one soldered joint. This appears to be most troublesome where the sub-panels (prefixed M) join the main part of the decoder.

CHAPTER SEVEN

The Colour Tube and its Ancillaries

The majority of dual-standard colour sets use the 19 or 25 inch size of tube. In either case the e.h.t. potential is 25kV., and that for the focus electrode around 4-5kV. These voltages are obtained from the line output transformer (as mentioned earlier) by the use of valve or solid-state rectifiers. In the case of valves shunt stabilisation of the e.h.t. is employed, using the PD500 which was specially developed for the job. It is this valve and the associated rectifier (GY501) that are responsible for the X-radiation which makes it essential for them to be enclosed in heavy-duty screening. The solid-state e.h.t. rectifier, often referred to as a tripler needs no stabiliser, and thus sets employing them do not have the X-ray problem.

The focus voltage is sometimes obtained, in valve stages, by the use of a bleeder network of high valve resistors from the main e.h.t. supply. An alternative is a separate valve or solid-state rectifier fed from the fly-back voltage appearing at the anode of the line output valve. It is then possible to effect control of the focus by varying the fly-back voltage by means of a pre-set potentiometer.

Sets using triplers frequently have the latter tapped to provide the necessary focus potential. This is normally applied to a metrosil resistor forming part of a high-voltage pot. The whole is enclosed in a plastic case to prevent flash-overs, etc.

Colour tubes are provided with means of varying the A1 potential in order that the three colour gunes may be balanced to give the correct range of colours. These controls are commonly fitted on the convergence panel, and fitted with switches to enable just a single colour to be displayed for setting-up purposes. However, one or two firms did not adhere to this practice and used either one switch for the blue gun alone (GEC) or none at all (Decca). This is sometimes a little inconvenient when adjusting colour purity, for which individual colours are called for. More of this later.

The scan coils used with the shadow-mask c.r.t. are larger versions of those for monochrome sets. They look a lot more complicated because they are in unit with the convergence coils, which latter have rather a lot of connections. They are in the shape of a broad inverted Y, with the windings on its legs. At the extremes are small circular magnets, rotatable about their axes. The coils effect dynamic convergence, the magnets static. Behind the convergence yoke, as it is called, are two disc magnets similar to the shift controls on a mono. tube. These are for achieving purity – i.e., to ensure that only electrons from the red gun fall on red dots on the screen, and so on.

There is one more assembly on the neck of the tube. This lies between the purity magnets and the base, and is called the blue lateral control. It is simply two coils with adjustable cores fed from the convergence network, and its function is to move the blue beam in the horizontal plane. Vertical movement is effected by the static magnet at the top of the yoke. Those on the other two arms are for red and green, working around clockwise.

The next item is the degaussing coils, discussed in Chapter Three. They are attached to a metal shield which fits around the body of the tube. They require no attention and are extremely reliable.

Finally we have the drive controls, with which the amount of colour drive from the colour difference amplifiers to the guns may be pre-set. They may consist of small pots., or of a system of flying leads to a group of sockets.

It is not usual to provide adjustment for all three guns, the red normally receiving full drive. To cater for the odd occasion when the latter may need to be altered some makers provide a means of transposing (say) the blue and red drives.

Once again not all manufacturers have adopted the common practice of mounting the drive controls on the tube base. Decca for instance, have them on the decoder board.

In the next chapter the order and methods of setting the various controls will be discussed.

Manual De-gaussing. As a preliminary to any adjustments concerning the c.r.t., many service manuals refer to manually demagnetising it by the use of a de-gaussing coil. In practice this action is only called for when the tube has been subjected to a really strong magnetic field, such as would occur if a loudspeaker were left close to it for some time. A suitable coil can be made by winding about 1000 turns of 31 guage enamelled copper wire on a 15 inch diameter former; but if you pause to consider this, you will realise that it entails over half a mile of wire! This is rather daunting in terms of effort and expense, so if manual degaussing is absolutely essential, it would certainly be easier to borrow a coil for the occasion.

To use it correctly, switch it on and move it over the front, top, and sides of the set (not the rear) ending with it parallel to the screen and some inches distant. Draw it away from the screen steadily to at least 8 feet distant, turn it vertically through 90 degrees, and switch off.

Note that de-gaussing coils are meant to be switched on only for short periods – not more than a few minutes in any hour. Longer running will cause them to overheat rapidly, with possible damage to the insulation. For this reason they are normally fitted with a type of mains switch which has to be held in the "on" position by the operator.

At one time it was thought that de-gaussing would be needed if the colour TV was so much as moved across a room. As with some other notions, possibly based on experience in the U.S., this proved a groundless fear.

CHAPTER EIGHT

Setting up the Picture

(1) Static Convergence and Purity

Start by running the set for about a quarter of an hour to ensure that it is fully warmed up, and that everything has "settled down". Then work with either Test Card "F" or a cross-hatch pattern on the screen.

For static convergence only the central part of the screen is important. When using the test card this is represented by the noughts and crosses on the blackboard. These, or the centre squares of the cross hatch should be white. If there is considerable colour fringing, adjust as follows:

Switch off the blue gun to leave the red and green only visible. Turn the appropriate static magnets slowly to overlay the two colours exactly. Switch on the blue gun and bring it into alignment by means of the static magnet and the blue lateral control.

Repeat as necessary to achieve optimum results.

Switch off or turn down both the blue and green guns. With a blank raster, advance the red screen control for moderate brightness. Inspect the raster for purity, i.e., for patches of other colours, or of a weaker shade of red. If these are present, partly release the wing nuts which secure the scan coils in their housing and slide them back towards the base of the tube. Rotate the purity rings individually, or as a pair. until you get a ball of red in the centre of the screen. Then slide the scan coils forward again until the screen is uniformly red. This may require some small readjustment of the rings. Once it has been achieved, tighten the wing nuts and switch in turn to the green and blue rasters. Slightly readjust the rings to move any small discrepancies. Finally check the red once more.

(2) Line and Frame Shift

This is best carried out using the test card. The shift controls are commonly located in or around the line transformer can. Adjust them to centralise the test card on the screen. Should the range of adjustment be insufficient, you may find that means are provided to reverse the sense of the controls. This takes the form of reversible plugs or flying leads and sockets.

The castellations around the edge of the test card should all be visible, fully so on the sides, but only half at the top and bottom. Reset the height and width controls, or the frame linearity if need be.

(3) Dynamic Convergence

Whilst the basic ideas are similar, each maker's practical layout and instructions for adjustment of dynamic convergence are quite unique. It is therefore not possible to quote a general method as with static convergence, and the service manual must be closely followed during the procedure. Note, however, that the instructions for the 405 system no longer apply, and may be ignored. In many instances the switching for the two convergence networks will have been fixed in the 625 position, often by the switch contacts having been soldered together. If this has not been done, it could pay you to delay carrying it out until you have had a try at convergence. On odd occasions the 405 network may give better results than the 625!

When it is completely redundant, parts from the 405 network (especially preset pots.) may be used to replace faulty items on the 625. The values of pots. are seldom greatly different. Speaking of these, it quite frequently happens that the optimum point of adjustment lies just outside the range of a pot, giving the impression that if only one could turn it a little more perfection could be achieved. In this case it may help to replace the control in question by one with a slightly higher resistance, e.g., from 200 ohms to 250. I have tried this dodge several times with success.

Not all the dynamic convergence controls will be pots. Some will be coils with variable cores. As always, the correct tool must be used for adjustment. In some sets, notably GEC, trimming tools were permanently attached to the cores.

Do not be too surprised to find that some of the controls do not do exactly as they should, according to the manual. In fact some may do the opposite! Hence the need sometimes to compromise.

There is also considerable discrepancy in the ease with which different sets may be converged, even to examples of the same model. One may seem to "click" into position, whilst another may take hours of patient work. One thing is certain, the need to realise when enough is enough. A desire to improve matters beyond an acceptable stage may lead to an awful lot of wasted time and effort. Remember that what may appear to be serious errors on a stationary test pattern viewed at close quarters can be virtually un-noticeable on a moving picture at a normal distance. If overall convergence is absolutely impossible to achieve, ensure that the middle of the screen, rather than the outer edges, has the best of the bargain. The action of most films and plays is concentrated within the centre section, and often the only time poor convergence outside it is noticed is when the credits are shown.

(4) Grey Scale and Drives

Now that you have a viewable picture on the screen, it may become apparent that there is a bias towards one colour, and that a background intended to be dark is not the neutral tint that it should be. The remedy for this condition is to set the Grey Scale, as it is called.

Darken the room by drawing the curtains or switching off artificial lighting. Turn the colour control to minimum, so that the set displays a black and white picture. (In certain sets some colour is present even at the lowest setting; slightly detune the set to remove this.) If a generator giving a stepped grey scale, or test card "F" is viewed, the various steps should be distinct and of the correct shade. If not, set the brightness control to about the three-quarter mark, and adjust the red, green and blue screen controls to obtain a picture that has the correct grey, and a normal level of brightness.

Examine the sections of the screen having the highest white tones. If these still show slight discolouration, the c.r.t. drive controls must be reset. These are frequently located on the tube base itself, taking the form of small preset pots, or alternatively plugs and sockets. Sometimes only the green and blue drives are adjustable, the red being permanently at maximum. Gradually reduce the dominant drive until the white is free of tinting; but if this happens to be red, and there is no control to alter, you may find that increasing the other two drives will do the trick.

As each drive control is altered, the screen controls will probably have to be readjusted to maintain the correct black level.

Finally, turn up the colour control to its normal setting, whereupon you should have well balanced, natural picture. If you are unfortunate enough to still have incorrect colours, it may be that one or more of the guns in the c.r.t. is low-emission. This condition produces an effect easily distinguished from that caused by a decoder fault-for instance, turning the brightness up and down on a poor tube will cause marked colour changes. The tube tester will readily confirm or allay your suspicions here.

Focussing is best carried out on the test card, since the setting which gives the most defined horizontal lines is not necessarily that which will produce the best definition on an actual picture. As with convergence, the centre portion of the screen is more important than the outer edges.

CHAPTER NINE

Spare Parts for your Colour TV

1. Valves. The most common types to be found in hybrid colour sets are as follows:

Type	Used As
ECC82	Frame oscillator.
PCL84	Colour difference amplifier.
PCL85	Frame osc/output.
PCL86	Sound amp/output.
PL508	Frame output.
PL509	Line output.
PY500	Booster diode
PCF80	Sync. seperator.
PCF802	Line oscillator.

Others are:

DY86/87/802	Focus rectifier.
GY501	EHT rectifier.
PD500	EHT stabiliser.

All these are obtainable from "surplus" stores at very reasonable prices. In addition, any non-working sets you may be able to buy cheaply should have their valves removed and tested in a good set, then stored for future use. Throw the bad ones away immediately, because if they hang around your bench for a long time you may forget that they were faulty, and give yourself unnecessary work when using them as replacements. Worse, valves with heater to cathode shorts can cause others to burn out, so take no chances!

2. Transistors. Although there are a fair number of different types to be found in the various makes of sets, in a lot of cases the BF115 or the BC108 are effective replacements. It's a good plan to keep half-a-dozen or so of each by you, and obtain the more expensive special types as and when needed. This applies in particular to frame and (in the Thorn 2000) line output transistors. The video amplifier transistors, too, in this chassis are a little more costly as they have to work with quite high collector voltages.

There must be literally dozens of firms advertising surplus transistors, as a glance through any TV magazine will confirm. My advice is to find a reliable supplier, and stick to him, even if his prices are slightly higher. Only recently I bought a quantity of BF115s at an attractive price, only to find later that most of them were shorted internally collector to emitter. The financial loss was small, but the cost in wasted time is another matter altogether! Since then I have taken to doing the simple base-collector-emitter test with the Avometer on every transistor before fitting them.

Returning to the subject of high power transistors, always search for any cause of the original's failure. Very often a driver transistor (again likely to be a BC108) which goes open circuit is responsible for the larger device drawing high collector current until the inevitable burn-out. Bias resistors should also be tested in case the heavy current has either made them change in value, or go completely open.

3. Line output transformers. Reference has already been made in Chapter 4 to the possible short-comings of non-standard replacements. In certain cases, of course, it may prove impossible to obtain transformers from the set maker, either because of obsolescence or due to a policy of not supplying anyone but an authorised dealer. If you experience the latter, it may be possible to order a spare through a local agent. Costs vary quite amazingly from one manufacturer to another; whilst preparing this book I had cause to buy two differing types, the dearer of which cost over £8 more than the other. This was in the trade price, so the cost to a retail customer would show an even more marked disparity.

If the maker has declared a certain model to be obsolescent, and cannot supply a replacement, it may pay you *not* to turn immediately to the specialist suppliers. First browse through all the finely printed adverts in "Television", "Wireless World", etc. It would appear that job lots of older spares must be sold off to various "surplus" dealers, and you may be lucky enough to locate a brand new transformer for a fraction of its original price.

Should a fellow-enthusiast own a similar model set to yours, and is amenable to the idea, it is a tremendous help to swop over the line transformers as a cross check. Having to unsolder and remake a large number of joints is tedious, true, but worthwhile if it saves you from spending £10 or more on an unnecessary replacement.

4. Miscellaneous components. Where resistors or capacitors have failed due to their working tolerances having been rather too low for their job, use higher-rated replacements. This is seldom difficult, since modern components tend to have better wattage-dissipation or voltage-working specifications for a given size than their predecessors. In most instances figures are quoted in service manuals, especially where close-tolerances are involved. It is also a good idea to refer to modification lists, where these are included, in case the value or rating of components has been altered to enhance reliability or performance.

Once again the choice of suppliers is extremely wide; and once again the old adage of not spoiling the ship for a ha'porth of tar is apt.

EHT triplers show almost as wide a variation in price as do line output transformers. Here too, a study of the surplus market can be rewarding. As an example, one very well known maker's genuine article can be had for less than one third of the trade price of a "special" replacement!

Scan coils, frame output transformers, mains droppers and transformers seem to be very durable indeed, and seldom need attention. In the rare cases where trouble is experienced, replacements should present no problem, as these items are pretty well standard.

APPENDIX ONE

A Combined Tester/Rejuvenator for CRTs

Simple rejuvenators for monochrome tubes have been around for some time. The basis of most is to apply a positive voltage to the grid of the tube with respect to the cathode – i.e., the opposite way to normal. This tends to remove impurities from the cathode and to restore its emission, often with a remarkable effect on the pictures produced.

The voltage required is about 200, plus of course 6.3 a.c. for the tube heaters. Common practice is to derive the h.t. directly from the mains using a silicon rectifier, followed by a current limiting resistor, which can conveniently be a 10 or 15 watt mains bulb. When the rejuvenation process is complete enough current flows through the bulb to light it, thus giving visual indication. The heater volts may be supplied by a small transformer or by dropping the mains by a rectifier/resistor combination.

The drawback of this otherwise useful little unit is its inability to actually test tubes; and since those with fairly good emission may suffer rather than benefit from the treatment, this can be a serious defect. A means of measuring the emission would enlarge the scope of the device enormously.

With this in mind I set about finding a way of testing tubes which would not involve a lot of complication and expense. At the same time it was clear that extending the capability to include colour tubes was also desirable, so this too was an aim from the start.

The emission of a tube, just as a valve, can be found by supplying it with a certain h.t. voltage via a meter. The current drawn will be related to the "goodness" of the tube. Unfortunately this would require the use of some 15kV for a black-and-white tube, and no less than 25kV for a colour type, to simulate working conditions! A less hazardous method had to be discovered!

All modern tubes have a number of electrodes in addition to the cathode, grid, and final anode. The extra ones are referred to as A1, A2, A3, and so on. A1 normally operates with upwards of 300v applied, derived from the boost h.t. line. The current consumed is small, but still proportional to the tube's emission. The manufacturers are curiously shy about quoting figures for A2 currents, so after ploughing through a large number of data books I conceded defeat and to determine it empirically. More of this later.

In order to cater for colour tubes a heater transformer capable of delivering 1 amp. was necessary, along with switching to enable each of the colour guns to be measured in turn. And common to these and monochrome tubes would be a switch to select "Test" and "Rejuvenate".

An obvious choice for the transformer was the type used in small tape recorders, etc., some years back, delivering 6.3. v.a.c. for the heaters and 200-250 for the h.t. It should be possible to acquire one of these from a scrap recorder or a surplus dealer at little cost. The gun selector switch is a two-pole four-way wavechange type. The Test/Rejuvenate switch is a 2-pole 2-way toggle, biassed to one position. (In case you are not familiar with this term, it simply means that an internal spring holds the switch firmly in one direction.) It is wired so its normal setting is "Test". Since it has to be held in the "Rejuvenate" position against the spring action there is no danger of accidentally leaving a tube "cooking" until it is rendered useless.

The use of a mains bulb as limiter/indicator is retained. I was fortunate enough to have by me a panel-mounted lamp holder with a lens about 1" in diameter, taking a small Edison screw mains bulb rated at 200v 10w. This sort of thing makes for neatness, but if not available may be replaced by a 15w Pygmy lamp in a standard BC holder.

The next job was to determine what kind of meter would be needed. The power supply for the tester was hooked up temporarily, and applied to some tubes known to be in good condition, via an AVO meter to measure the A1 current. It appeared that the maximum would be less than 500 micro-amps, with a really low tube taking down to about 20. An 0-500 uamp meter would thus be ideal, at least as far as black-and-white tubes were concerned. Such a meter new would cost around £3.50, so once again a look around a surplus store is well worth while.

With the basis of the tester established practical construction work could begin. It was decided to mount all the components on a panel, which could then be placed in front of a suitable box. As it was available I used paxolin for the panel, and wood, covered with "Fablon" wood graining for the box, but aluminium for either or both sections would be quite in order. A suggested layout for the panel is shown in the diagram.

Mark the position and size of the various holes on the panel and drill them out carefully. If a circle or tank cutter is not available for the meter hole, use the old dodge of drilling small holes around the circumference, until the middle part can be broken out. Finish off with a half-round file to remove the "cogs" left behind.

Fit the meter, lamp, switches, and transformer, then screw two strips of soldering tags on the inside as suggested in the second diagram. The order in which you wire up the components is immaterial, but do

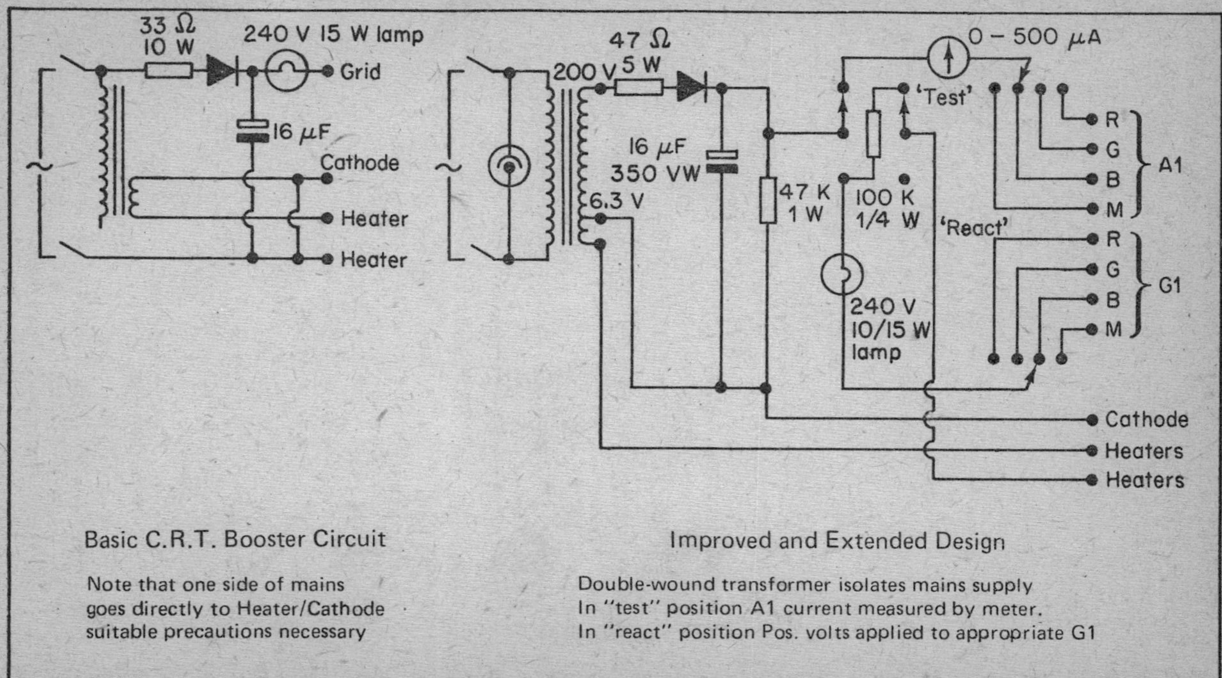

Basic C.R.T. Booster Circuit

Note that one side of mains goes directly to Heater/Cathode suitable precautions necessary

Improved and Extended Design

Double-wound transformer isolates mains supply
In "test" position A1 current measured by meter.
In "react" position Pos. volts applied to appropriate G1

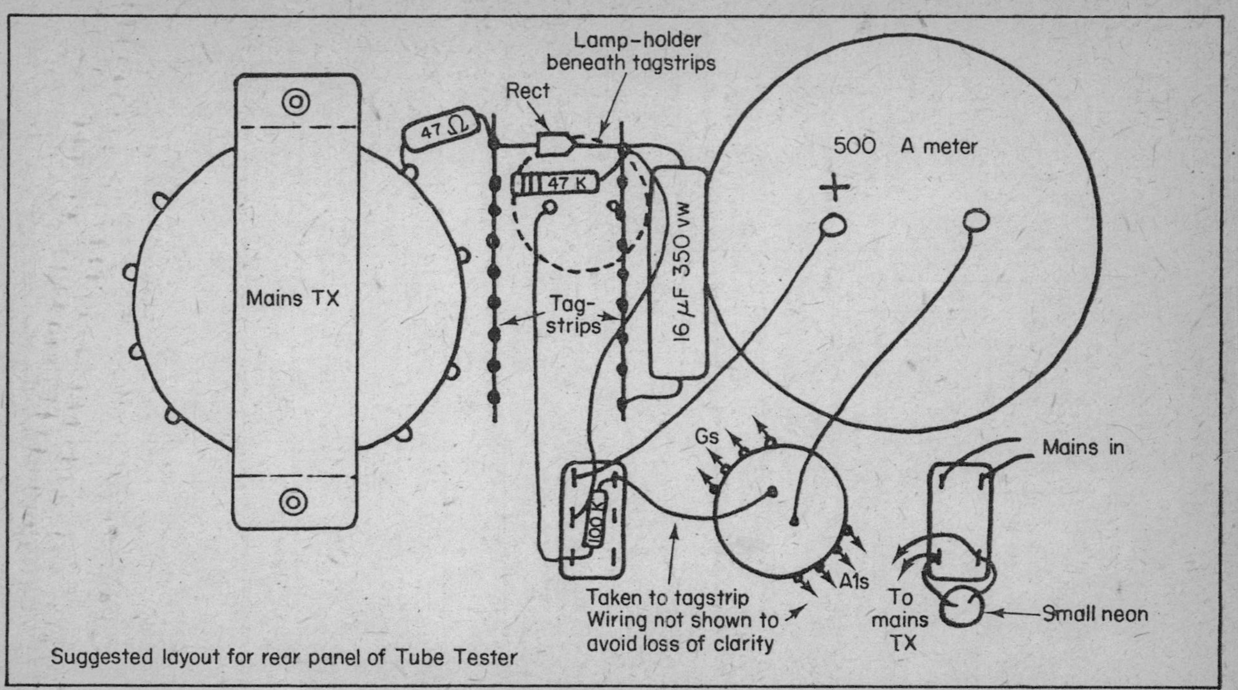

Suggested layout for rear panel of Tube Tester

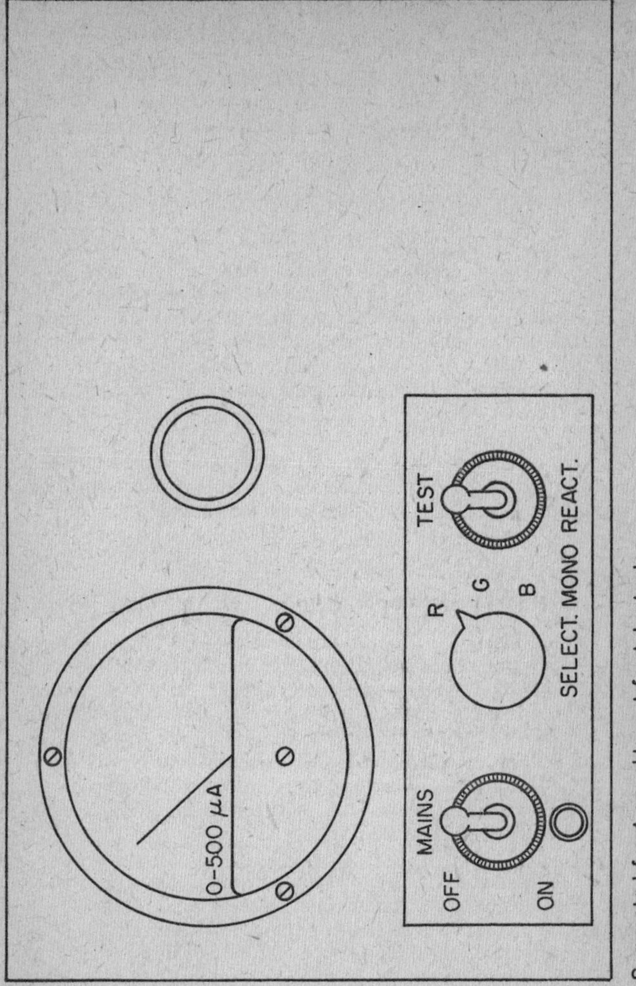

Suggested front panel layout for tube tester.
Lettering by dry-transfer method

take great care when working on the Red/Blue/Green/Mono switch. It is all too easy to make a mistake which would result in the instrument not testing or rejuvenating the indicated gun.

A ten-way cable is required to connect the completed instrument to the two test tube bases. I used two 3-core and two 2-core flexes to obtain the ten cores cheaply. The four flexes were laid carefully together and bound with cloth tape, giving a neat and durable appearance. The 3-core cables will have either red/black/green or brown/blue/green colouring according to age; either presents a convenient coding for the three colour guns. Connect the R/B/G grids and A1s to their respective switches with these cables. The three colour cathodes, and that of the mono base are all connected to each other and the earthy side of the heaters. The latter are supplied by one of the 2-core flexes, using the red or brown core as live. The remaining 2-core has its red or brown and black or blue cores connected respectively to the mono. A1 and grid.

The test bases are obtained from scrap sets. In both cases Bush/ Murphy types are very suitable, as they have rather large paxolin surrounds fitted with useful soldering points. Remove all the original components before attaching the test cables. The two bases may then be fitted back to back, using metal or paxolin stand-offs about 1½" long. Secure the cables to one of the fixing bolts so that the soldered joints do not take any strain.

When a metal panel and/or box is used, employ three-core flex for the mains lead, and ensure that there is a reliable connection to the earth core in the instrument. The small neon indicator is a precaution against the mains being left switched on accidentally.

Use of the Tester/Rejuvenator

1. Mono. tubes. Fit the appropriate base and switch on, with the gun switch in the mono. position. The meter should start to read within about two minutes, unless the tube is exceptionally "lazy". A reading of over 150 uamps will normally mean that the emission is enough to produce a reasonable picture. It must be stressed, however, that variations in HT voltage will affect the A1 current, and it is advisable to employ the method mentioned earlier, with some good tubes, to get a norm for your particular instrument. Very low readings indicate that the rejuvenation treatment is called for.

Hold the switch in the "Rejuvenate" position. The meter is automatically switched out of circuit, and will read zero. If the tube responds well the 10 or 15 watt indicator lamp will soon start to glow, and perhaps achieve almost full brilliance. As soon as this occurs release the switch into the test position, and check the meter reading. If it exceeds your norm, leave well alone. Attempting to increase the emission still further may have the reverse effect. An exception to this is when the meter reading drops back after a few seconds. When this happens an alternative method of rejuvenation often works well. Instead of holding the switch down, flick it very quickly, so that a sharp pulse of voltage is delivered to the grid. This may have to be repeated many times before an acceptable and steady reading is obtained

Tubes treated by the instrument have their useful life extended significantly in most cases. Generally speaking, the worse a tube is to start with, the better the results.

Now and again you may get hold of a tube which just will not improve. This is more than likely because the treatment has been applied previously, and tube cathodes just don't seem to like a second spring cleaning!

2. Colour Tubes. When evaluating the A1 current of good and bad colour tubes to obtain working averages, I found that the readings differed much more than with mono. tubes. Low emission c.r.t.s. could register as little as 25ua., whilst new one would send the meter right off scale. Since the majority of tubes tested were hardly likely to be in the latter category, this was not a major problem.

One of the most useful aspects of being able to check the emission of the three guns separately is the case with which one can decide if the lack of a colour or colours is due to a decoder fault or the tube itself. Each gun should draw substantially similar A1 current, whether or not the level of emission is high or low. The discovery that one or other is very low will save hours of trying to achieve a satisfactory grey scale.

In most instances it has been my experience that the "quick flick" method works best when rejuvenating. This sometimes has a most remarkable effect, with a reading shooting up from little or nothing to right off scale. Usually I am content to get anything above 200ua. This will provide good watchable pictures. British and European tubes seem to be amenable to treatment, but I must confess that the few Japanese types I have tried have been none too successful. Maybe the Orientals have found a way of building in obsolescence!

APPENDIX TWO

A Simple Crosshatch Generator

When this book was first conceived BBC2 transmitters were operating throughout the working day, radiating Test Card F between the few public programmes and the series of trade test films. There was, thus, ample opportunity for the enthusiast to converge a colour TV on the test card, without having to obtain a costly crosshatch generator. Unfortunately the need for economy has forced the BBC to close the second network between programmes, and the amount of time that the test card is to be seen on BBC1 and ITV is limited by the increased number of daytime programmes. In any case, the person able to work only in the evenings would be severely handicapped by the lack of a test card, or a generator. For these reasons the need for a simple type of instrument has become very urgent.

Professional generators are expensive items. Their small physical size belies the complexity of the circuitry inside. There has to be an oscillator covering Bands 4/5 (and sometimes Band 3 as well) with either continuous or pre-set tuning. This is modulated by the cross-hatch wave-form for injection into the aerial socket of the set under test. The signal must include sync. pulses to lock the pattern on the screen. In addition to the crosshatch, most generators provide a dot pattern and some kind of grey scale. To construct such an instrument in the home workshop would be very difficult and costly.

In practice, however, a straightforward crosshatch pattern alone would be sufficient for the enthusiast. The dots are intended for setting up static convergence, but this is seldom difficult without this facility. Similarly, grey scale is easily achieved by the means described in Chapter Eight of this book. The omission of these functions from the generator would simplify it immediately. Further economies can be made by injecting the signal not as modulated r.f., but as a video wave-form directly into the luminance amplifier; and by finding another method of synchronising.

Firstly, suitable pulses for triggering and synchronising a test pattern are available from the line output transformer of a colour TV, via the same windings which supply the decoder panel. Secondly semi-conductors are cheaply and easily obtained, with which a physically small and inexpensive generator may be constructed. In the last year or so some examples have appeared commercially using integrated circuits of the TTL (transistor-transistor logic) type. In these the line pulses are sampled, divided and sub-divided to give the necessary wave-forms. This certainly makes for a very small unit, but for various reasons a different approach, using discrete components, is a more attractive proposition for the enthusiast.

I believe that one of the foremost considerations in preparing a design for the home constructor is that the component parts should be readily at hand, so that there should be a minimum of delay in completing the project. Again, these parts should be easily tested and replaced should a fault occur. Integrated circuits, excellent though they might be, present a serious problem in this respect. Unless a check list of voltages is provided for correct operating conditions it is not possible to test an integrated circuit; the only sure method is to replace it with another. This may be acceptable in workshops where spares are available "off the shelf"; but not so good for the enthusiast who may have to wait a considerable time for delivery by post.

It would not be practicable to build a generator using i.c.s. without a printed circuit board, but the most elementary bread-board layout can be employed for the discrete component type. My prototype was, in fact, constructed on a piece of scrap wood approximately 7" x 4" x ½", in a matter of three hours. Every part was taken from the "junk" box. The cost was minimal, and obviously replacements will not cause any anguish!

Circuit Description

To present a crosshatch pattern on the screen of the set we have to apply two suitable waveforms to the luminance amplifier grid (or base). These may be easily generated by multivibrators closely resembling the bi-stable used in the colour decoder panel. The output from the multivibrators is taken to twin amplifiers which sharpen it into a sawtooth shape. The signals are then combined and fed to the set via a short length of co-ax cable. The only other connection is the sync. input feed, which goes to the burst gate pulse on the decoder panel.

Constructional Notes

The layout shown in the diagram is merely suggested, and may be modified to suit individual ideas. The transistors used (2SB75) were to hand in large quantities from a dismantled computer, but any general purpose device should be satisfactory. N-P-N transistors will require the battery supply leads to be reversed. Likewise, the diodes are by no means critical, and any of the OA81 equivalent types may be used. The resistors were all of the 10% tolerance type, as were the capacitors in the verticals generator. (470 and 680 pf.) The corresponding components in the horizontals generator are best found by selection. The tolerance of capacitors of these values seems to leave a lot to be desired! The wide variation of actual capacity in those marked identically results in marked difference in the number of lines displayed.

The battery supply can be between 4.5 and 9 volts, without alteration of circuit values or performance.

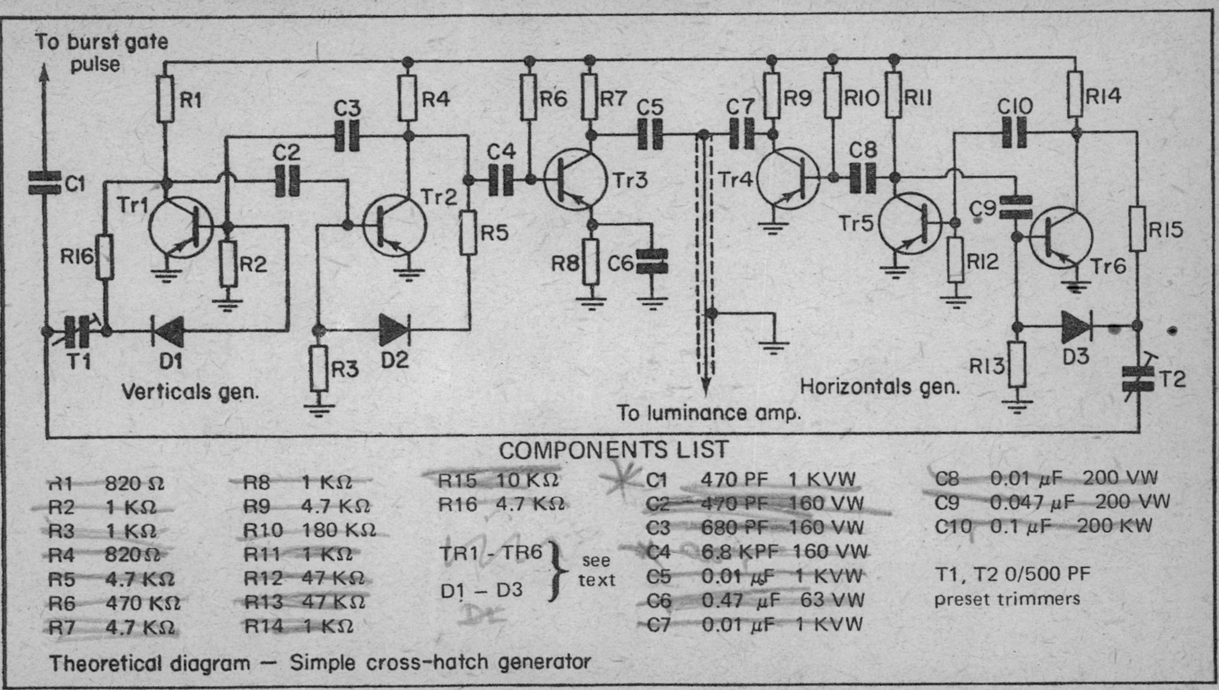

COMPONENTS LIST

R1	820 Ω	R8	1 KΩ	R15	10 KΩ	C1	470 PF 1 KVW	C8	0.01 μF 200 VW
R2	1 KΩ	R9	4.7 KΩ	R16	4.7 KΩ	C2	470 PF 160 VW	C9	0.047 μF 200 VW
R3	1 KΩ	R10	180 KΩ			C3	680 PF 160 VW	C10	0.1 μF 200 KW
R4	820 Ω	R11	1 KΩ	TR1 - TR6	see text	C4	6.8 KPF 160 VW		
R5	4.7 KΩ	R12	47 KΩ			C5	0.01 μF 1 KVW	T1, T2 0/500 PF	
R6	470 KΩ	R13	47 KΩ	D1 – D3	see text	C6	0.47 μF 63 VW	preset trimmers	
R7	4.7 KΩ	R14	1 KΩ			C7	0.01 μF 1 KVW		

Theoretical diagram — Simple cross-hatch generator

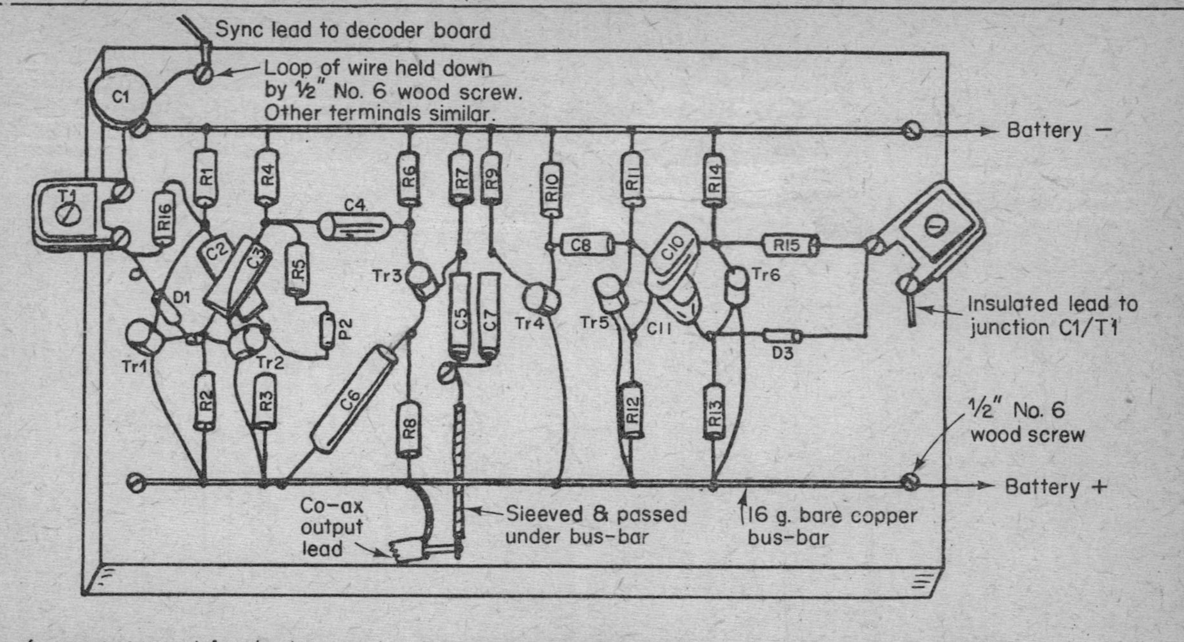

Suggested layout for simple cross-hatch generator

Operation. Many sets already have test points at the luminance amplifier input and on the decoder, to which the generator connections may be made. If these are not present, however, it is suggested that short lengths of fairly thick wire be soldered to the printed board at the appropriate places to receive crocodile clips.

With the video input and line pulse connections made, switch the TV on and allow it to warm up. Switch on the crosshatch generator, whereupon some sort of pattern should appear on the screen. Adjust the verticals sync. trimmer for stable lines, then that for the horizontals. Best results will probably be obtained by having the set tuned to a station, and reducing the contrast until the pattern over-rides the picture. Finding the correct adjustment for the second trimmer can sometimes be a little tricky, but with practice you will soon be able to master it.

Convergence may then be carried out in accordance with the general remarks earlier in this book, and with the manufacturers instructions.

Note. Values given for components are not especially critical. Individual experiment is permissible, and indeed may result in interesting variations of the vertical/horizontals ratio.

APPENDIX THREE
Foreign TV Reception on Your Colour TV

Many readers will be aware that under certain conditions reception of continental TV stations becomes possible. The normal line-of-sight restrictions on range are suspended, due to a number of various causes. The most familiar manifestation of this is the heavy patterning on British Band 1 stations in hot weather. Sometimes this is so severe as to obliterate the pictures altogether, and whilst the ordinary viewer is cursing heartily, the DX enthusiasts are having a ball!

For many years the "standard" receiver for long distance TV was the good old Bush TV53 series. The line time base of this 405 only set could be induced to scan at 625 lines merely by fiddling with the line hold control. (Continental stations mostly use this standard.) The change from negative to positive modulation which is also required is very easily accomplished by reversing the connections to the vision detector. But the most useful feature was the tuner unit. This resembled a conventional 13-channel type from a casual glance at the knobs, but was in fact completely different. Tuning was by moving brass cores within long narrow coil formers. A single wafer switch gave selection of Bands 1 or 3. Movement of the cores was effected by a series of cams on the rear of the channel-change knob, whilst the fine tuner simply varied the cores by a small amount. Thus the coverage of the two Bands was continuous, unlike the preselected frequencies of the turret type, and ideal for tuning in Continental stations. (Their vision channel E2 is pretty well the same as our Channel 2 sound. A turret "biscuit" could hardly be expected to tune this successfully.)

Now that colour is being radiated by a large number of Continental Band 1/3 stations, it is quite possible to receive them successfully in this country. Owners of sets imported from Germany and Austria often have nothing else to do but to switch their tuners from UHF to VHF and connect a Band 1, or even a Band 2 aerial to the set to get foreign pictures in colour. The author has a friend who has received many programmes this year in this way, and who has photographs and colour slides to prove it!

Should you wish to have a go at this fascinating hobby – be warned, it's a real time-waster! – you can convert your dual-standard colour TV with very little effort.

It should not be difficult to acquire a Bush tuner unit from a scrap set. Countless thousands must now be lying idle around workshops and junkrooms. The object is to wire it into the set in such a way that it is in circuit in place of the UHF tuner when the set is working on 625 lines. The power requirements are simple enough, 16v at 0.3a for the heaters and around 200v for the h.t. The former may be obtained by tapping into the heater chain at a convenient point, or by the use of a small transformer. There are numerous points from which the h.t. voltage may be drawn, but probably the best is one with a fair amount of decoupling. In sets using a valve sound output the "hot" end of the output transformer is an ideal source. The i.f. output lead from the new tuner takes the place of that from the original.

Don't expect to switch on and get pictures instantly. This can happen, of course, but very often a great deal of patience is required before the first alien test card flashes up on your screen. If the line and frame hold controls are left as they were for UHF reception, little or no adjustment should be necessary on VHF. Signals strong enough to provide a viewable picture will lock it in automatically.

As mentioned earlier, a Band 1 or 2 aerial will often give good results. To achieve good pick up in most directions, a Channel 1 or 2 X aerial mounted horizontally works well. Naturally very sophisticated systems are available should you wish to go to extremes. I must confess to feeling that some of the fun goes out of a hobby when it is taken too seriously!

You will probably want to make a record of your "catches" by photographing them. The best camera for the purpose is the single lens reflex, with the twin lens version second. With both of these one can focus the image accurately upon the viewing screen, thus ensuring sharp pictures. Simpler cameras with means of focusing may also be used, provided that the distance between the film (i.e. the rear of the camera, not the lens) is measured carefully. Since you will be at or near the shortest focal length to fill the viewfinder with the image of the TV screen, it is better to use a tape measure rather than depend upon a range-finder. Remember also that the phenomenon of parallax error occurs at close quarters, meaning in simple terms that the image in the viewfinder may be some inches disposed from that on the film. This may be avoided by ensuring that the centre of the camera lens is directly opposite to that of the TV screen.

In all cases a tripod should be used to support the camera. Once the correct position for this is found some means of finding it quickly again is advisable if it is not possible for it to remain untouched. Use a fairly long cable release to operate the shutter. This will not only avoid camera shake, but also allow you to sit back from the screen in comfort.

As for film and shutter speeds, and apertures, the choice is pretty straightforward. In the days when I used to take a lot of shots in black and white, FP3 film, rated at 200 ASA and exposed for 1/25 sec. at f.4.5 gave me excellent negatives. The processing was done at home and under my control. Now that colour rules, and slides and prints are done commercially, I use 100 ASA film shot at 1/25 or 1/30 sec at f2.8. It is permissible to use longer exposures, say 1/15 or even 1/10 sec. if the picture is steady enough, but never go above 1/30. At faster speeds the camera will perceive what your eye cannot and reproduce split images and other weird effects.

The golden rule is to shoot whenever an acceptable picture arrives. Don't wait for it to improve, as the chances are that it might disappear! And you can always take a second exposure if there is a marked improvement.

Set the brightness and contrast controls to give a not-too contrasty picture. Try to avoid ambient lighting falling upon the screen by having the set in a shaded place and drawing the curtains when there is strong sunlight.

With a little luck and perseverance you should be able to log and photograph a number of stations. Not all will be receivable in colour, but, as stated earlier, you will probably find yourself devoting an awful lot of time to the attempt!

—— · —— · ——

BP1	First Book of Transistor Equivalents and Substitutes	60p
BP2	Handbook of Radio, TV and Ind. & Transmitting Tube & Valve Equiv.	60p
BP6	Engineers and Machinists Reference Tables	50p
BP7	Radio and Electronic Colour Codes and Data Chart	25p
BP11	Practical Transistor Novelty Circuits	40p
BP14	Second Book of Transistor Equivalents	1.10p
BP22	79 Electronic Novelty Circuits	1.00p
BP23	First Book of Practical Electronic Projects	75p
BP24	52 Projects using IC741	95p
BP25	How to Build Your Own Electronic and Quartz Controlled Watches & Clocks	85p
BP26	Radio Antenna Handbook for Long Distance Reception & Transmission	85p
BP27	Giant Chart of Radio Electronic Semiconductor & Logic Symbols	60p
BP28	Resistor Selection Handbook (International Edition)	60p
BP29	Major Solid State Audio Hi-Fi Construction Projects	85p
BP30	Two Transistor Electronic Projects	85p
BP31	Practical Electical Re-wiring & Repairs	85p
BP32	How to Build Your Own Metal and Treasure Locators	1.00p
BP33	Electronic Calculator Users Handbook	95p
BP34	Practical Repair & Renovation of Colour TV's	1.25p
BP35	Handbook of IC Audio Preamplifier & Power Amplifier Construction	1.25p
BP36	50 Circuits Using Germanium, Silicon and Zener Diodes	75p
BP37	50 Projects Using Relays, SCR's and TRIAC's	1.25p
BP38	Fun & Games with your Electronic Calculator	75p
BP39	50 (FET) Field Effect Transistor Projects	1.25p
BP40	Digital IC Equivalents and Pin Connections	2.50p
BP41	Linear IC Equivalents and Pin Connections	2.75p
BP42	50 Simple L.E.D. Circuits	75p
BP43	How to make Walkie-Talkies	1.25p
BP44	IC 555 Projects	1.75p
BP45	Projects on Opto-Electronics	1.25p
BP46	Radio Circuits using IC's	1.35p
BP47	Mobile Discotheque Handbook	1.35p
BP48	Electronic Projects for Beginners	1.35p
BP49	Popular Electronic Projects	1.45p
BP50	IC LM3900 Projects	1.35p
BP51	Electronic Music and Creative Tape Recording	1.25p
BP52	Long Distance Television Reception (TV–DX) for the Enthusiast	1.45p
BP53	Practical Electronic Calculations and Formulae	2.25p
BP54	Your Electronic Calculator and Your Money	1.35p
BP55	Radio Stations Guide	1.45p
BP56	Electronic Security Devices	1.45p
BP57	How to Build your own Solid State Oscilloscope	1.50p
BP58	50 Circuits using 7400 Series IC's	1.35p
BP59	Second Book of CMOS IC Projects	1.50p
BP60	Practical Construction of Pre-Amps, Tone Controls, Filters and Attenuators	1.45p
BP61	Beginners Guide to Digital Techniques	95p
BP62	Elements of Electronics – Book 1	2.25p
BP63	Elements of Electronics – Book 2	2.25p
BP64	Elements of Electronics – Book 3	2.25p
BP65	Single IC Projects	1.50p
BP66	Beginners Guide to Microprocessors and Computing	N.Y.A.
BP67	Counter Driver and Numeral Display Projects	N.Y.A.
BP68	Choosing and Using Your Hi-Fi	N.Y.A.
BP69	Electronic Games	N.Y.A.
126	Boys Book of Crystal Sets	25p
160	Coil Design and Construction Manual	75p
196	AF–RF Reactance – Frequency Chart for Constructors	15p
200	Handbook of Practical Electronic Musical Novelties	50p
201	Practical Transistorised Novelties for Hi-Fi Enthusiasts	35p
202	Handbook of Integrated Circuits (IC's) Equivalents and Substitutes	1.00p
203	IC's and Transistor Gadgets Construction Handbook	60p
205	First Book of Hi-Fi Loudspeaker Enclosures	75p
207	Practical Electronic Science Projects	75p
208	Practical Stereo and Quadrophony Handbook	75p
210	The Complete Car Radio Manual	1.00p
211	First Book of Diode Characteristics Equivalents and Substitutes	1.25p
213	Electronic Circuits for Model Railways	1.00p
214	Audio Enthusiasts Handbook	85p
215	Shortwave Circuits and Gear for Experimenters and Radio Hams	85p
217	Solid State Power Supply Handbook	85p
218	Build Your Own Electronic Experimenters Laboratory	85p
219	Solid State Novelty Projects	85p
220	Build Your Own Solid State Hi-Fi and Audio Accessories	85p
221	28 Tested Transistor Projects	95p
222	Solid State Short Wave Receivers for Beginners	95p
223	50 Projects using IC CA3130	95p
224	50 CMOS IC Projects	95p
225	A Practical Introduction to Digital IC's	95p
226	How to Build Advanced Short Wave Receivers	1.20p
227	Beginners Guide to Building Electronic Projects	1.25p
228	Essential Theory for the Electronics Hobbyist	1.25p